SUPER INTERESTING FACTS FOR SMART KIDS

JORDAN MOORE

AMARYLLIS

AMARYLLIS
An imprint of Manjul Publishing House Pvt. Ltd.
• C-16, Sector 3, Noida, Uttar Pradesh 201 301, India
Website: www.manjulindia.com

Registered Office:
• 2nd Floor, Usha Preet Complex, 42 Malviya Nagar,
Bhopal 462 003 – India

Distribution Centres
Ahmedabad, Bengaluru, Chennai, Hyderabad,
Kochi, Kolkata, Mumbai, Noida, Pune

Super Interesting Facts For Smart Kids by Jordan Moore

This paperback edition first published in India in 2025

ISBN 978-93-5543-498-2

Printed and bound in India by Repro India Limited

CONTENTS

INTRODUCTION

Did you know that St Barbara is the patron saint of firefighters and miners?

Or that your eyes blink around 20 times every minute? Generally, each blink has an interval of 2-10 seconds.

Or that snakes smell with their tongues?

Or that William Shakespeare—perhaps the world's most famous writer, spelled his own name six different ways? There are 80 recorded ways to spell Shakespeare.

And did you know koalas sleep for up to 20 hours every day? Or that the world's biggest hotel has 7,351 rooms (Las Vegas of Asia)? Or that only around a quarter of the Sahara Desert is actually covered in sand?

The world is full of interesting things just waiting to be discovered. And if you like random facts like those, then you're in luck—because this book is full of more than 1,000 of them!

In fact, this book has precisely 1,272 facts, covering everything from the sun and the moon in outer space to the animals and plants here on Earth - plus food and drink, film and TV, words and languages, sports and games, and a lot more besides!

Some of these facts are funny.

Some of these facts are strange.

Some of them are surprising.

But all of them are SUPER INTERESTING!

To help you find your way around, all the facts in this book are divided into 12 different sections, each one covering a different subject—from the stars and planets to sports and games.

So, what are you waiting for?! Let's dive right into some SUPER INTERESTING facts for SMART KIDS!

SPECTACULAR SPACE

THE UNIVERSE

- There are 5 to 10 times more stars in the universe than there are grains of sand on all the beaches on Earth.
- Ninety-five percent of the universe is invisible because it is made of the mysterious "dark matter" and "dark energy" that does not interact with light.
- The universe is 13.8 billion years old plus or minus about 130,000 years, more than twice as old as the Earth, which is estimated to be 4.54 billion years old, plus or minus about 50 million years!
- The universe is estimated to be 93 billion light-years wide.
- The distance of the sun to the earth is approximately 8.3 light minutes away from Earth.
- The universe is constantly expanding. If we were to try to travel to the edge of it, the edge would keep moving away from us so it would be impossible to get there!
- Space is almost completely silent.
- Approximately 73% of the mass of the visible universe is in the form of hydrogen.

Helium makes up about 25% of the mass, and everything else represents only 2%.

- The galaxy in which the Earth is found—the Milky Way—is thought to contain as many as 200 billion stars.
- There are 9 galaxies visible to the naked eye that you might see when observing the sky, and there are about 13 nebulae that you might see.
- Until the 1920s, scientists believed the Milky Way was the only galaxy in the universe. We now know ours is one of hundreds of thousands of different galaxies!
- Scientists have found an enormous cloud of water vapor floating in space 10 billion light years away. The water cloud is estimated to contain at least 140 trillion times the amount of water in all the seas and oceans here on Earth.
- If two pieces of metal were to touch in outer space, they will bond and be permanently stuck together; this amazing effect is known as cold welding.
- It would take 400 million years for a standard spacecraft to travel to the center of the Milky Way. Even if you could travel at the speed of light (300,000 kilometers, or 186,000 miles, per second), it would take you about 25,000 years to reach the middle of the Milky Way.

- The biggest asteroid in our solar system is 329 miles in diameter.
- In 2019, scientists took a photograph of a black hole for the first time. It is 3 million times larger than the Earth! This black hole is 6.5 billion times the mass of the Sun.
- The Earth orbits the Sun in one year—but it takes the Sun around between 225 million and 250 million years to orbit the Milky Way!

THE SUN

- The Sun is really a gigantic star. It only looks so much bigger and rounder than the other stars we can see because it is so much closer to the Earth.
- The Sun is 13 billion times brighter than the next brightest object in the sky, the star Sirius.
- The Sun is a million times larger than the Earth. It holds 99.8% of the solar system's mass and is roughly 109 times the diameter of the Earth.
- ...and about one million Earths could fit inside the sun!
- It takes light from the Sun eight minutes to reach Earth.
- Like the Earth, the Sun rotates anticlockwise in space.
- The Sun produces its own winds, which blast from its surface at speeds of more than 300 miles per second! The solar wind can reach speeds of approximately 155-466 miles per second and is supersonic.
- Every second, the Sun converts around 4 million tons of matter into energy.

- The amount of energy the Sun produces in one second is equivalent to the power of 100 billion tons of dynamite!
- The Sun is thought to be 4.5 billion years old...
- ...and it will stop burning in around another 4 billion years' time.
- The Sun makes up 99.9% of all the mass in our solar system.
- Unlike the Earth, the Sun is almost perfectly round.
- It takes tens of thousands of years for energy produced at the Sun's center to reach its surface.
- The surface temperature of the sun is estimated to be 10,000 °F...
- ...while the temperature at its core reaches 27 million °F!

THE STARS

- The stars in the night sky are grouped together into 88 different constellations.
- Not all our constellations are visible at the same time. Some of those in the northern hemisphere cannot be seen in the south, and some in the south cannot be seen in the north!
- The largest constellation in the night sky is called Hydra. It takes up around 3% of the night sky...
- ...while the smallest constellation, Crux, takes up just 0.2%!
- Smaller groups of stars than constellations are called asterisms. Orion's Belt—a group of three stars inside the constellation of Orion—is one.
- Constellations travel from east to west across the sky, just like the Sun.
- Almost all the stars you can see in the night sky will be brighter than our sun. They don't look as bright because they're so far away!
- Light from distant stars takes so long to reach Earth that some of the stars we can see in the sky will actually no longer exist...
- ...and there are some stars that we will never be able to see at all!

- There is a star called Lucy in the constellation Centaurus that scientists believe has a gigantic diamond at its center! Lucy's physical composition—primarily carbon and oxygen, with a thin layer of hydrogen and helium—is typical of a white dwarf, which is what remains of a star after it exhausts its nuclear fuel and dies.
- Special stars called neutron stars are so dense that a single teaspoonful of them may weigh the same as all of the people on Earth.
- Although most stars are round, like the Sun, a star called Vega—one of the brightest stars in the northern sky—is squashed and bulges out at its center like a melon! There is flattening at its poles and its equator is extended, giving Vega the shape of an oblate spheroid. The star is 23 percent wider at the equator than at the poles.
- Stars don't actually twinkle. It's the gases in the Earth's atmosphere that make the light from them appear to flicker in the sky.
- A person with good eyesight on a clear night can see around 2,000 stars...
- ...the furthest and faintest of which will be around 20 million billion miles away!

THE MOON

- Although it looks round to us, the Moon is actually shaped more like a lemon and bulges out at its north and poles.
- Only 12 people have ever set foot on the Moon...
- ...and no one has been there since 1972.
- There were once active volcanoes erupting on the Moon.
- Some of the objects left behind on the Moon by astronauts that have been there including golf balls, a family photograph, a copy of the Bible, a toy astronaut, a hammer, and a feather.
- There is no wind on the Moon...
- ...so the footsteps of the astronauts who have landed on it will remain there for hundreds of thousands of years!
- The Moon is thought to have once been a part of the Earth. It broke away a long time ago when our planet was still a swirling ball of liquid rock.
- Australia is wider than the Moon.
- The craters of the Moon's south pole are some of the coldest places in our entire solar system because they're permanently in shadow as a result of the low angle at which sunlight

strikes the Moon's surface in the polar regions (and also because the Moon has no atmosphere to help warm up its surface).

- All the planets in our solar system could fit end to end between the Earth and the Moon.
- The gravitational pull of the Moon is what gives the Earth's oceans their tides.

- Some scientists think the Earth may once have had two moons, but they bumped into one another and joined together, leaving us with the one we have today!
- The Moon experiences moonquakes, just like the Earth experiences earthquakes.

THE PLANETS

- Jupiter is more than twice the size of all the other planets in our solar system added together. Jupiter's immense volume could hold more than 1,300 Earths.
- The biggest volcano in the solar system is called Olympus Mons. It is found on Mars and it is the largest volcano in the solar system at 72,000 ft tall (two and a half times the height of Mount Everest) and 374 miles wide (nearly the size of the state of Arizona). It is three times the size of Mount Everest!
- The Earth only has one moon—but all the planets in our solar system put together have over 200 in total...
- ...82 of which belong to Saturn alone!
- Neptune is so far away that it gives off more heat than it receives from the Sun.
- Mercury is so close to the Sun that sunlight would be seven times brighter than here on Earth, and the Sun would appear three times larger in the sky.
- Venus is the hottest planet in our solar system. Its surface temperature is approximately 869 °F—that's hot enough to melt lead!

- The Earth is the only planet in our solar system not named after one of the gods that the Ancient Greeks and Romans believed in.
- The air pressure on the surface of Venus is 92 times that on Earth. In fact, it's more like the pressure you'd find at the bottom of the ocean.
- Sunsets on Mars are blue.
- Venus rotates backwards, in the opposite direction to the other planets in our solar system...
- ...while the planet Uranus rotates on its side!
- Mars is the only planet other than Earth that has human technology on its surface.
- While one year on Earth lasts 365 days, one year on Mercury lasts only 88 days.
- Gravity is $2\frac{1}{2}$ times stronger on Earth than it is on Mars. The surface gravity on Mars is only about 38% of the surface gravity on Earth, so if you weigh 100 pounds on Earth, you would weigh only 38 pounds on Mars.
- Winds on Neptune blow at more than 1,500 mph.
- Mercury is the fastest planet in our solar system. It travels around the sun at 30 miles every second!
- The atmosphere of Venus is made up of thick clouds of toxic gas and sulfuric acid...

- ...so if you were to visit it, the entire planet would smell like rotten eggs!
- Iron rocks and minerals on the surface of Mars rust like metal in the planet's atmosphere, turning it a dull red color -which is why it's called the Red Planet!
- Jupiter turns on its axis every ten hours, but it takes 12 years to completely orbit the Sun. So a year on Jupiter would appear to last more than 10,000 days!
- Earth is the only planet in the solar system to have liquid water on its surface...
- ...but the surface of Mars has frozen ice caps just like Earth, and even frozen areas of salt water. Scientists think that it was once covered in vast oceans and seas, just like our planet.
- The stripes and patches on the surface of Jupiter are actually gigantic clouds...
- ...while its famous red spot is an enormous swirling hurricane. The storm is so large that it could engulf the entire Earth!
- Venus rotates very slowly. A single day there would last the same as 243 days here on Earth!
- Although they look solid, the rings of Saturn are actually made of millions of clumps of ice and rock.

- Because it takes 165 years to orbit the Sun, the planet Neptune has only completed one full orbit since it was first discovered in 1846.
- The dwarf planet Pluto has an oval-shaped orbit, so sometimes it is closer to the Sun than Neptune!
- When the British astronomer William Herschel discovered Uranus in 1781, he wanted to name it after the King of England at the time. If he had got his way, it would have been called Planet George!

SPACE TRAVEL

- The word astronaut literally means "sailor of the stars". It is a person trained as a cosmonaut to travel in space.
- The first person in space was the Russian astronaut Yuri Gagarin in 1961...
- ...who was followed by the first woman in space, Russia's Valentina Tereshkova, in 1963.
- The first drink ever consumed in outer space was Coca-Cola.
- It costs NASA $15-22 million to make one astronaut's space suit.
- There is a patch of Velcro on the inside of an astronaut's helmet so that the wearer can scratch their nose!
- One of the astronauts who went to the Moon on the Apollo 17 mission discovered he was allergic to moondust (Harrison Jack Schmitt's mission in 1972).
- It would be impossible to write in space using a normal pen because gravity affects the flow of ink to the nib. Astronauts have to take special writing tools with them to write things down while in space. The Russians used pencils to overcome this problem.

- Because of the lack of gravity, astronauts grow around 2 inches in height while they are in space.
- Astronauts on the International Space Station recycle their water by filtering their pee! It takes around eight days to fully clean it, but the water they end up with is so pure that it is actually cleaner than tap water here on Earth!
- Animals were sent into space long before the first humans...
- ...In fact, among the first creatures to be sent into orbit were fruit flies, monkeys, mice, dogs, cats, rats, rabbits, frogs, and a guinea pig.
- When Neil Armstrong landed on the Moon in 1969, it was estimated that 600-650 million people watched it live on television.
- To read the instruction manuals on the International Space Station, astronauts from all countries that visit it have to learn to speak some Russian.
- Space suits are exceedingly difficult to wear on Earth because they weigh more than 120 kg!
- Showers and baths are impossible in space, so astronauts have to clean themselves with a damp soapy washcloth.

- In 2021, 90-year-old *Star Trek* actor William Shatner became the oldest person to go into space.
- When he retired in 2004, John Young became the longest-serving astronaut in the history of space travel. In total, he had worked in space flight at NASA for 42 years!
- Spacecraft need to withstand extreme temperatures. While in space, the temperature outside can drop to -454 °F, but when the spacecraft re-enters the Earth's atmosphere, it reaches more than 2,192 °F!
- The longer they are in space, the weaker astronauts' bones become.
- Powered food, like salt and sugar, is not permitted on the International Space Station because the individual grains would float away and could get into the machinery on board. Instead, foods are seasoned with flavored liquids.
- Astronauts train for walking in space by striding through swimming pools wearing space suits.

OUR WONDERFUL WORLD

THE EARTH

- The Earth is estimated to be over 4.54 billion years old.
- The Earth is the third planet from the Sun. That makes it not too hot and not too cold—perfect for us to live on it!
- It is 93 million miles from the Earth to the Sun. That distance is known as an astronomical unit.
- The Earth isn't round, but more egg-shaped. Its actual shape is properly known as an "oblate spheroid".
- One day is the time it takes the Earth to turn around completely. It actually takes slightly less than 24 hours. The earth rotates once every 23 hours, 56 minutes and 4.09053 seconds.
- The Earth spins through space at around 1,000 mph...
- ...and here on the surface, you would move faster the closer to the equator you are!
- All the continents of the world were once joined together as one single landmass called Pangea.
- 90% of all the fresh water on Earth is frozen solid in the Arctic and Antarctica.

- Antarctica was completely ice-free until around 34 million years ago.
- Although we need oxygen to breathe, the Earth's atmosphere is mostly made of nitrogen. It also contains tiny amounts of many other substances, including gases—neon, helium, and methane.
- Water covers about 71% of the surface of the Earth...
- ...but only around one-fifth of that water has ever been visited by humans.
- The Earth is very gradually slowing down. Every century, a day on Earth gets around 2 milliseconds longer...
- ...but when the Earth was first formed, a day was only six hours long!
- In Antarctica, the number of residents varies, from around 1,100 in the harsh Antarctic winter to around 4,400 in the milder summer months of October to February, plus an additional staff of 1,000 in the nearby waters.
- The inside of the Earth is made up of different layers. We live on the outer layer, called the crust, which floats on top of a layer of molten rock, called the mantle, beneath which is a solid core.

- The center of the Earth is hotter than the surface of the Sun.
- Although the Earth's crust is rocky, the commonest substance in the Earth's crust is actually a gas: oxygen.
- There is enough gold inside the Earth to coat the entire surface of the planet, the thickness would be somewhere between 6 inches and two *feet.*
- The Earth has different seasons because it is slightly tilted. The northern hemisphere is tilted toward the Sun during summertime, and away from the Sun in the winter...
- ...which is why the northern and southern hemisphere experiences their seasons at opposite times!
- Every 250,000 years or so, the Earth's magnetic north and south poles change places.
- There is twice as much water vapor in the air by the sea than inland.
- Because the Earth's atmosphere becomes thinner the higher you go, three quarters of its mass lies within 7 miles of the surface.

RIVERS, LAKES, AND WATERFALLS

- Africa's River Nile is the world's longest river. It runs for more than 4,000 miles through 11 different countries!
- A swimmer named Martin Strel swam the entire Mississippi River in 2002. It took him 68 days!
- Lake Baikal in central Russia is the oldest, second largest, and deepest lake in the world. It contains more water than all the Great Lakes of North America put together.
- The Mississippi River has one of the largest river basins in the world. Although the river itself flows through only ten American states, it collects water from more than 30!
- Lake Tanganyika is the second largest lake in Eastern Africa. It is so big that it is divided between four different countries.
- Despite its name, the Dead Sea in the Middle East is actually a small lake. It is so salty that it is almost impossible to swim or dive into it...
- ...and in fact, water in the Dead Sea is more than nine times saltier than the water in the sea!

- The island of New Guinea in Indonesia is so wet that its longest river, the Fly, carries more water than all the rivers of Australia combined! With a mean annual discharge of approximately 6,000 cumecs, the Fly is similar in size to the Niger and Zambesi Rivers in Africa and the Danube in Europe.
- The world's second longest river is the Amazon in South America...
- ...but no one knows for sure exactly how long the Amazon is, because not all of it has been explored!
- Australia's longest river, the Murray, provides enough water for 1.5 million homes.
- Niagara Falls produces 25% of all the power used by the state of New York and the Canadian province of Ontario.
- Angel Falls in Venezuela, South America, is the world's tallest waterfall. The height is 3,211 ft and the plunge is 2,648 ft.
- The world's deepest river is the Congo, in central Africa. Parts of it drop to more than 720 ft below the surface—more than twice the height of the Statue of Liberty!
- 10% of all the surface fresh water on Earth is held in America's Lake Superior...

- ...which contains more water than all the other four Great Lakes of North America combined!
- In fact, there is enough liquid in Lake Superior to cover all of North and South America in 1 ft of water!
- Inga Falls in Africa is the world's most powerful waterfall. More than 91 cubic ft of water flows over it every second!
- South America's Río de la Plata River is only 180 miles long—shorter than the River Thames in London—but it drains water from a basin more than 1.2 million sq. miles in size!
- It takes three months for the water to flow the entire length of the Mississippi River.
- Khone Falls in the Asian country of Laos is the world's widest waterfall. From one side to the other it measures on average 35,376 feet.
- Europe's Danube River flows through more capital cities than any river in the world. From one end to the other, it flows through Vienna in Austria, Budapest in Hungary, Belgrade in Serbia, and Bratislava in Slovakia.
- Loch Ness in Scotland is so deep that it contains more water than all the other lakes in Britain put together!
- England's River Thames is crossed by more than 200 bridges along its entire length.

- The Mississippi is one of the world's widest rivers. At its broadest point, it is 11 miles from one bank to the other.
- The Rhine-Main-Danube Canal is a vast series of waterworks connecting western Europe's River Rhine to the River Danube in the east. The joining between them effectively makes everything to the west of the canal—including much of France and Spain—into an island!

MOUNTAINS AND VOLCANOES

- No one can quite agree on at what point a hill becomes a mountain!
- ...But most scientists take any land that rises over 1,000 ft or more above sea level to be officially a mountaintop.
- And if that were the case, then one-fifth of the surface of the Earth is covered by mountains!
- The world's longest mountain range is actually underwater. The Mid-Ocean Ridge runs for 40,390 miles around the Earth, following fault lines in the plates of the Earth's crust.
- The world's highest mountain, Mount Everest, is 29,031ft tall. And...
- ...it's getting taller! Mount Everest is growing by around an eighth of an inch every year.
- More than 6,000 people have climbed Mount Everest, and dozens more complete the climb every year.
- Fourteen of the world's highest mountains are found in the Himalayas, the same mountain range as Mount Everest.
- Mount Kea in Hawaii is 4,000 ft taller than Mount Everest—but its base is below the sea!

- Some birds that live in India have to migrate over Mount Everest in the spring!
- Gangkhar Puensum in Bhutan, a tiny country in Central Asia, is the world's 40th highest mountain—but at 24,836 ft it is the tallest mountain that has not been climbed.
- America's Rocky Mountains form the longest mountain range in the world. It runs for more than 3,000 miles from Alaska to Mexico.
- Parts of the Rocky Mountains are over 80 million years old!
- In 2015, scientists at the United States Geological Survey discovered that America's highest mountain, Denali, was actually 10 ft taller than they had previously thought!
- Some of the tallest mountains in Antarctica are actually enormous snow-covered volcanoes. The largest, Mount Sidley, is dormant—but the second largest, Mount Erebus, is still active, and was probably erupting when it was discovered in 1841!
- The Alps mountains in central Europe lie across the borders of seven different countries: France, Italy, Switzerland, Germany, Liechtenstein, Austria, and Slovenia.
- There are 82 volcanoes in Europe—32 of which are found in Iceland. Most of which are not monitored.

- There are 1,350 active volcanoes around the world, aside from the continuous belts of volcanoes on the ocean floor.
- ...not all of which are on land! Some volcanoes are encased below in ice in the Arctic and Antarctic, and some of them are completely submerged and lie on the seabed.
- The Pacific Ocean is surrounded by an enormous chain of active volcanoes known as the Ring of Fire.
- Molten rock is called lava when it is ejected from a volcano but is called magma when it is inside the Earth.
- Around the world, one in every 20 people lives within an area that could be affected by a volcanic eruption at any time!
- Lava thrown from a volcano is more than 1,832 °F!
- The world's tallest volcano is Mauna Loa in Hawaii. It is 13,677 ft tall.
- The loudest sound ever produced in nature was a volcanic eruption. When Krakatoa in Indonesia erupted in 1883, the sound was heard 3,000 miles away!
- When a volcano erupts, it can affect an area as large as 20 miles around it!

- Australia is the only continent in the world with no active volcanoes.
- When a volcano erupted on the tiny island of Tristan da Cunha in 1961, the entire population was moved to England! Most families returned in 1963.

DESERTS

- A desert is any area of land that receives less than 10 inches of rain in a year.
- The Sahara Desert is said to be the world's largest desert. It covers 8% of the entire surface of the Earth...
- ...but because it is too cold for any kind of rain or snow to fall, Antarctica is technically the world's biggest desert—because it fits the definition too!
- Although it is mostly inhospitable, approximately 626,161 people live in the Sahara Desert.
- The world's driest desert is the Atacama Desert in South America. On average it receives less than 1mm of rain every year...
- ...and in some parts of the Atacama, it hasn't rained for more than 500 years!
- Desert sand dunes shift with the wind and can move by several feet every year.
- The highest mountain in the Sahara Desert is actually a volcano. It is called Emi Koussi (11,204 ft) and is in the north African country of Chad.

- Only around a quarter of the Sahara Desert is actually covered in sand. The rest is rocky and covered in large areas of stone or gravel.
- In fact, only around 20% of the world's deserts are sandy!
- Half of the Sahara Desert receives less than an inch of rainfall in an entire year.
- Some of the sand dunes in the northern Sahara Desert are more than 1,300 ft tall.
- The word Sahara means "desert" in Arabic—so the Sahara Desert is literally the "desert desert"!
- There are actually lots of lakes and pools of water called oases in the Sahara Desert. But most of them contain saltwater, like the sea, so we cannot drink from them.
- The Gobi Desert in Asia has one of the most extreme climates anywhere on Earth. In summer, the temperature can rise to more than 53 to 93 °F—but in winter can fall to 27.5 °F!
- Because of the extreme temperatures, most animals that live in the desert are nocturnal and only come out at night.
- Areas of a desert that are covered in sand that can be blown by the wind are called ergs...

- ...one of the largest of which is found in the Arabian Desert and is called The Empty Quarter.

FORESTS

- 30% of the Earth is covered in forest.
- Half of the world's forests are found in just five countries: Russia, Brazil, Canada, the USA, and China.
- 80% of all the animals and plants in the world are found in forests.
- The Earth's forests are believed to contain approximately 3 trillion trees—half of which are in the rainforests.
- The vegetation that grows in the middle layer of the forest is called the "understory" and the floor of a forest is called the forest floor.
- There are more than 100 different tribes living in the forests of Brazil that have never been contacted by outsiders.
- A healthy 100-foot-tall tree has about 200,000 leaves. A tree this size can take 11,000 gallons of water from the soil and release it into the air again, as oxygen and water vapor, in a single growing season.
- A single hectare of tropical rainforest can contain nearly 500 different types of trees...
- ...while the Amazon alone is home to 2.5 million distinct types of insects!

- Forests help to fight climate change because trees soak up the excess carbon dioxide in our atmosphere.
- In parts of Central Asia, people who live in forests force trees to grow into living bridges!
- There is a pine tree in Nevada in the western United States that is believed to be more than 5,000 years old. When it first started to grow, Stonehenge would just have been built!

OCEANS AND SEAS

- The Pacific Ocean covers 60 million square miles, making it by far the world's largest ocean.
- In fact, the Pacific Ocean alone covers almost a third of the Earth!
- The Pacific is also the world's deepest ocean. The Mariana Trench, near the Philippines, drops to almost 36,201 ft.
- Because all five of the world's oceans—the Pacific, Atlantic, Indian, Southern, and Arctic—flow into one another, some scientists say that the world has only one "World Ocean".
- Around three-quarters of all the oxygen, we breathe is produced in the oceans.
- Only around 5% of the world's oceans have been explored by people.
- All the oceans of the world contain more than 300 million cubic miles of water.
- The oceans are home to 95% of all the animal life on Earth.
- Because sunlight cannot shine any more than 330 ft below the surface of the water, most of the ocean is completely dark.

- There is an underwater canyon in the Bering Sea in the North Pacific Ocean that is 2,500 ft deeper than the Grand Canyon!
- In some places, heat from inside the Earth escapes into the bottom of the ocean. The water around these places can be superheated to more than 750 °F!
- Scientists think the water in the Earth's oceans could contain around 20 million tons of gold...
- ...while there is enough gold in the seabed to give everyone in the world $250,000 worth!
- The world's largest sea is the Philippine Sea. It covers 1.9 million sq. miles!
- Twenty-two different countries have a coastline on the Mediterranean Sea.
- The Pacific Ocean is wider than the Moon.
- A single iceberg can contain approximately 20 billion gallons of water.
- Because Canada has so many islands, it has more coastline than any other country—almost 125,567 miles!
- Four in ten of all people in the United States live by the coast.
- There are thought to be three million shipwrecks at the bottom of the world's oceans.

- If all the ice in the world were to melt, the sea level worldwide would rise by more than 250 ft.
- The Caribbean is one of the world's deepest seas. At its lowest point, it is 25,217 ft deep...
- ...which means the Caribbean is deeper than the world's shallowest ocean—the Arctic! The average depth of the Arctic Ocean is 3,953 feet and it is 18,264 feet at its deepest point.

ISLANDS

- At more than 770,000 sq miles, the world's largest island is Greenland. But if you consider Australia as an island, it is the largest at 2,969,976 sq. miles.
- The island that is home to the most people in the world is Java in Indonesia. It has a population of 141 million people!
- Roughly one in six people in the world live on an island.
- Madagascar is the world's oldest island.
- In fact, Madagascar has been on its own for so long that 90% of all the animals and plants that live there are now found nowhere else on Earth!
- The tiny Mediterranean island of Malta has no rivers and was denuded by the Knights Crusaders, but trees have since been replanted.
- More than 850 different languages are spoken on the island of New Guinea.
- A group of islands is called an archipelago.
- The Isle of Dogs in London isn't actually an island at all—in fact, it is attached to the English mainland!
- Some islands are manmade.

- Hawaii is the only US state to be entirely made of islands. As a result...
- ...it is the only US state with no straight lines on its borders!
- At 21,000 sq. miles, Devon Island in the Canadian Arctic is the largest uninhabited island in the world.
- Hawaii is continuously volcanic. As the lava from its volcanoes cools and forms rock, the islands expand by around 40 acres every year—that's the same as 20 football pitches!
- The largest island in the Caribbean is Cuba.
- The largest island in the Mediterranean Sea is Sicily, off the south coast of Italy.
- The Caribbean Island of St. Lucia is the only country in the world named after a woman.
- Indonesia is the largest country in the world made up entirely of islands. In 2017, the Indonesian government tried to count the number of islands it has but stopped counting at 17,508!
- Stockholm, the capital city of Sweden, is built across 14 different islands. The Stockholm Archipelago has over 24,000 islands.
- The island of Ilha da Queimada Grande, off the coast of Brazil, is home to so many snakes

that the Brazilian Navy has had to stop people from going there!

- More than 400 people on Japan's Okinawa Island are over 100 years old. It means that one Japanese person in every 1,450 is now aged over 100.
- Until around 50,000 years ago, the island of Flores in Indonesia was home to a population of small humans, called Homo Floresiensis. All of them were less than 4 ft tall.
- The island of La Gomera in Africa's Canary Islands is so mountainous that the locals developed a language of loud whistles to make themselves heard from one valley to the other.
- According to Greek mythology, Zeus—the king of the gods—was born on the island of Crete.
- The largest island in the United States is called Big Island. It's in Hawaii.
- Rockall is a tiny rock in the middle of the Atlantic Ocean, around 320km (200 miles) off the coast of Scotland. Although it is technically uninhabitable, in 2014, the explorer Nick Hancock lived on the island for 45 days!

THE WEATHER

- The coldest temperature ever recorded on Earth was -128.6 °F at the Soviet Vostok Station in Antarctica.
- Lightning burns at around 50,000 °F...
- ...and in fact, a single bolt of lightning can heat the air around it to a temperature five times hotter than the surface of the Sun!
- The hottest temperature ever recorded was 134 °F in a place called Death Valley in California, USA.
- On 14 January 1972, the temperature in the town of Loma in Montana, USA, went from -53 °F one day, to 49 °F by the following day. The difference of 103 °F is the biggest shift in temperature ever recorded!
- Large raindrops fall to the ground at around 20 mph.
- The earthy smell in the air after a heavy rainstorm has a name! It is called petrichor.
- The winter of 1684 was so cold in England that the River Thames froze solid for two months.
- The USA has more tornados per year than anywhere else.

- The wind is formed by the air in the Earth's atmosphere trying to balance out areas of high and low pressure. As the air moves from high-pressure areas to low-pressure areas, we feel the movement as wind.
- In 1995, more than 8 ft of rain fell in the town of Cherrapunji in India in two days.
- In the winter of 1971–72, more than 93.5 ft of snow fell on Mount Rainier National Park in the USA. It is officially the snowiest place in the world!
- The heaviest hailstones ever recorded fell in Bangladesh in 1986. They weighed around 2.5 lbs each and were the size of grapefruits!
- The winds inside a tornado blow at over 300 mph.
- The largest tornado ever recorded was more than 2.6 miles across. It struck the town of El Reno in Oklahoma, USA, in 2013.
- Sometimes rain can evaporate before it even reaches the ground and disappears in midair.
- A lightning bolt stretching nearly 477 miles across three states now holds the record for the longest lightning flash. On 7 February 2022, the World Meteorological Organization announced that a single bolt on 29 April 2020 stretched over Texas, Louisiana, and Mississippi. At any given moment, there are

around 2,000 thunderstorms taking place around the world...

- ...and there are more than 40 lightning strikes every second!
- In some parts of India, the rain is sometimes bright red!
- The mouth of the Catatumbo River in Venezuela, in South America, is the stormiest place in the world. Every square kilometer in the area has more than 250 lightning strikes every year!
- In 1972, a blizzard in Iran lasted for a week and covered more than 200 villages in over 20 ft of snow!
- Crickets and grasshoppers chirp differently depending on the temperature outside.

AMAZING PLACES

COUNTRIES AND CONTINENTS

- The world's largest country is Russia. It covers more than 6.3 million sq miles—which is more than 11% of the entire land mass of the Earth.
- The world's smallest country is Vatican City, which covers less than 0.2 sq miles. It is so small that it is entirely surrounded by the city of Rome!
- Africa is divided into more countries than any other continent. In total, there are 54 of them!
- Brazil is so big that it shares a land border with all but two of the other countries in South America—Chile and Ecuador...
- ...in fact, Brazil alone covers almost half the entire area of South America!
- Of all the world's most powerful earthquakes, 18.5% happen in Japan.
- A country that has no coastline is called a landlocked country. Of all the people in the world, 7% live in a landlocked country.
- The world's largest landlocked country is Kazakhstan in Asia. It is approximately 1 million sq miles in size.
- 1.414 million people live in China—that's more people than any other country in the world!

- Mecca is the hottest city in the world. It is the warmest inhabited place on earth, with an average annual temperature of 87.3 degrees Fahrenheit. In summer, temperatures can reach 120 degrees Fahrenheit.
- Canada has more lakes than any other country.
- San Marino in central Europe is the world's oldest sovereign state. It has existed for more than 1,700 years!
- Ecuador in South America is named after the fact that it stands directly on the equator.
- The world's flattest country is The Maldives. Its highest point is just 16 ft above sea level—and is a manmade hill on a golf course!
- Turkey lies partly in Europe, and partly in Asia.
- Australia is the only country that is a continent and an island.
- China is so large that it spans five different time zones—but the entire country follows whatever the time is in the capital city, Beijing.
- Bolivia in South America has 38 official languages.
- Half the population of the African country Niger are under 16 years old.
- According to a 2022 survey, Finland is the world's happiest country. The least happy are in Afghanistan.

- More than a quarter of all the land in the Netherlands is below sea level, making it the lowest country in the world.
- The United States has more millionaires and more billionaires than any other country.
- Iceland is the official world's most peaceful country.
- The tiny country of Lesotho in southern Africa is the world's highest country. The lowest point you can go there is still more than 3,281 ft above sea level!

TOWNS AND CITIES

- There are more than 10,000 cities in the world with a population above 1 million.
- Istanbul is the only city in the world to straddle two continents: half of it is in Europe, the other half in Asia.
- The Japanese cities of Tokyo and Kyoto are anagrams: they are spelled using the same five letters, T, O, K, Y, and O. Tokyo took over from Kyoto as the capital of Japan in the 1800s.
- The Spanish Steps aren't in Spain—they're in Rome, Italy!
- Copenhagen in Denmark is the world's safest city as of 2021.
- Reykjavik, the capital city of Iceland, is the world's most northerly capital city.
- The world's most southerly capital is Wellington in New Zealand.
- Hong Kong in Asia is the most expensive city in the world to live in (2021).
- Nobody knows for sure what the name "London" actually means.
- New York was originally called New Amsterdam.
- The average tourist visiting Dubai will spend more than $500 every day!

- According to the United Nations, Tokyo is the world's biggest capital city. It is home to more than 37 million people!
- The world's smallest capital is Melekeok, the capital city of the Pacific Ocean Island nation of Palau. Only 250 people live there!
- In 2022, the city of Jacobabad in Pakistan became the world's hottest city. Temperatures there are often over 123.8 °F!
- Bangkok is now the world's most visited city.
- People have lived in the city of Jericho in western Asia for more than 11,000 years!
- The world's oldest capital city is Damascus, Syria, which was founded in 2500 BCE.
- The German city of Hamburg has more than 2,300 bridges.
- Eight hundred different languages are spoken in New York.
- Because the city is in the desert, all of the public fountains in Las Vegas use water recycled from people's bathrooms and kitchens!
- The official name of Bangkok has 168 letters! It is the longest place name in the world. (Krung Thep Maha Nakhon is the shortened version.)
- Murmansk in northern Russia is the largest city inside the Arctic Circle. Temperatures there often fall below -4 °F during the winter.

- There is an enormous underground lake in the middle of Paris!
- The capital city of Tajikistan, a country in Central Asia, is called Dushanbe. Its name means "Monday" in the local Tajik language because the city developed around a marketplace that opened on Monday mornings!

FLAGS

- When Alaska and Hawaii officially because US states in the 1950s, the US flag had to be updated to show 50 stars—one for each of the states. The design that was chosen was the work of a 17-year-old school student. He received a B- grade for his work!
- The flag of the United States has had to be updated 26 times in history—more than any other national flag in the world!
- The top lefthand corner of a flag—like where the stars on the Stars and Stripes of America—is called the canton.
- The flag of Switzerland is perfectly square.
- The national flag of Nepal is two triangles, one on top of the other. It is the only flag in the world that is not a square or a rectangle and is actually a pennant.
- The island of Bermuda has a picture of a shipwreck inside the shield on its flag.
- The red circle in the middle of the flag of Japan is meant to represent the sun.
- The flag of Albania has a two-headed eagle on it.

- Only two countries in the world have purple on their flag: Nicaragua in Central America and the Island of Dominica in the Caribbean.
- Denmark has used the same flag since 1219. It is the oldest flag in the world.
- Until 2011, the flag of Libya was completely green.
- Two countries have maps of themselves on their flags—Cyprus and Kosovo...
- ...while the island of Guam in the Pacific Ocean has the name "GUAM" written across it!
- In 2016, scientists in Waterloo, Canada, produced a copy of the Canadian flag that was 0.6 micrometers in size—that's about one-fifth the size of a strand of spider's silk!

NATIONAL ANTHEMS

- The UK's national anthem, "God Save the Queen," changes to "God Save the King" when there is a monarch is a man.
- The lyrics to the national anthem of Japan were written more than 1,000 years ago. *The lyrics* are based on a waka poem from the 10th century, sung to a melody composed by Hayashi Hiromori in 1880.
- Japan's national anthem is also the shortest in the world.
- The Spanish national anthem has no lyrics.
- ...and is also one of the oldest national anthems in the world. It has been used at official events in Spain since 1770!
- The national anthems of Finland and Estonia have the same tune...
- ...while the country of Liechtenstein uses the same tune as "God Save The Queen!"
- In 1993, the European country of Czechoslovakia split in two, to form two new countries, the Czech Republic and Slovakia. Rather than share the same national anthem, the Czech Republic took the first verse of the Czechoslovakian anthem, and Slovakia took the second!

- The first letters of each of the 15 verses of the Dutch national anthem spell out the name WILLEM VAN NASSOV, who was a famous figure in Dutch history.
- The tune of America's national anthem, "The Star-Spangled Banner," was originally a drinking song!
- The French national anthem, "La Marseillaise," is named after the city of Marseilles.
- The national anthem of Uganda has just eight bars of music!
- The national anthem of Jordan has just four lines...
- ...while the full version of the Greek national anthem has 158 verses (stanzas)!
- The national anthem of the island of St. Helena is called "My Saint Helena Island". It was written by an American man named David Mitchell who had never been there!
- The national anthem of South Africa has five different verses that are sung in five different languages.

BUILDINGS

- The world's tallest building is the Burj Khalifa in Dubai. It is 2,716 ft tall and has more than 160 floors!
- There is a building in Moscow State University in Russia that is said to contain a total of 33 kilometers of corridors and 5,000 rooms.
- Although we think of pyramids as being in Egypt, the African country of Sudan has more pyramids than any other country in the world!
- The world's first skyscraper was built in Chicago, USA, in 1885. It only had ten floors and was 138 ft high.
- The Restaurante Botín in Madrid, Spain, is the world's oldest restaurant. It opened in 1725!
- The Romanian parliament building in Bucharest is the world's heaviest building. It is so big and made of such thick stone that, in total, it would weigh more than 4 million tons!
- Mjøstårnet is the name of an 18-floor building in the town of Brumunddal, Norway. It is the tallest building in the world made entirely of wood at 280ft!
- The world's largest prison is Rikers Island Prison sitting on 413 acres of manmade island.

- The Temple of the Tooth is a famous Buddhist temple in Sri Lanka. It is traditionally said to be home to one of Buddha's teeth!
- Heavenly Jin is the name of a restaurant in Shanghai, China. It is located on the 120th floor of the Shanghai Tower, making it the highest restaurant building in the world.
- There are 775 rooms in Buckingham Palace in London—including 78 bathrooms!
- Buckingham Palace has six times more rooms than the White House.
- St. Peter's Basilica in the Vatican City is the largest church in the world and can house more than 60,000 people.
- The famous Leaning Tower of Pisa has always leaned. Even when it was still being built, the people constructing it noticed it was lopsided but never corrected it!
- NASA builds its spacecraft in an enormous hangar called the Vehicle Assembly Building. It is so huge that it has its own climate inside!
- There is a church in Taipei in eastern Asia that is shaped like a shoe.
- The British Library in London has more than 180 million different books and artefacts.
- The Grand Mosque in the city of Djenne in Mali, Africa, is over 278ft long—quite an

achievement considering the entire building is made from dried mud!

- In 2006, a house in Canada was picked up and moved 1,205 miles across the country!
- The Great Pyramid of Giza in Egypt was the tallest building in the world for 3,500 years.

TRANSPORT

- The world's first road maps were produced by the Romans more than 2,000 years ago.
- If you were to ride the entire length of Russia's enormous Trans-Siberian Express railway, you would cross 3,901 bridges.
- The Kolyma Highway (1262 miles) which connects the cities of Nizhny Bestyakh and Magadan in Russia -is the coldest road in the world. Temperatures often fall below -40 °F— but the lowest temperature recorded along the road's length was -89.9 °F!
- There are more than 4 million miles of roads in the United States...
- ...and more than 19,622 airports.
- Most of the London Underground network is actually above ground!
- The Eiksund Road Tunnel in Norway is the deepest road tunnel in the world. It drops 942 ft below the surface of the Earth!
- Dubai International Airport is said to be the busiest international airport in the world. It handles 9 million passengers every year!

- Highway 10—a major motorway in Saudi Arabia—is almost entirely straight. If you were to drive along it, you would not turn a corner for 158 miles!
- The steepest road in the world (Baldwin Street) is found in the city of Dunedin in New Zealand.
- Opened in 1936, the toll road leading up to the San Francisco-Oakland Bay Bridge in California has 23 lanes.
- Australia's Highway 1 encircles the entire country. At more than 9,000 miles, it is the longest unbroken road in the world!
- The two islands of Papa Westray and Westray in Scotland each have an airport. It takes just 96 seconds to fly from one to the other! The shortest record time is 53 seconds.
- There are no railways in Iceland.
- People in the United States take 10 billion bus trips every year.
- The Shanghai Maglev Train is the fastest train line in commercial service in the world. Trains travel along it at 286 mph!
- College Park Airport in Washington, United States, has been a working airport since 1909.
- The London Underground opened in 1863. It is the oldest underground system in the world.

- There is more than 135,000 miles of rail track in the United States—but less than 1% of it is electrified.

THE PECULIAR PAST

HISTORY

- The Persian and Roman Empires were at war with one another for 680 years.
- Alcohol was invented before the wheel.
- The Battle of Bunker Hill didn't actually take place on Bunker Hill. It took place across the Charles River in Boston.
- Banknotes were first produced in China, more than 1,500 years ago.
- The Aztecs used to use chocolate as money.
- In the 13th century, the pope declared war on cats...
- ...and in the 1930s, Australia went to war against emus!
- Napoleon Bonaparte, the famous leader of France, was once attacked by thousands of rabbits.
- The earliest boats were used by humans perhaps as many as 10,000 years ago!
- During the Second World War, the British government had lots of inflatable tanks placed along the south coast of England, to make it look like the coast was much more heavily defended than it really was!

- In 1867, an unopened bottle of Roman wine was found in Germany. It is around 1,700 years old—and because its seal is intact, it is probably still drinkable!
- When the Second World War ended, people in Russia celebrated for so long that the entire city of Moscow ran out of vodka. It is worth considering the fact that in wartime, the Soviet Union did not have large reserves of vodka.
- Oxford University was founded nearly a thousand years ago, in 1096.
- A polar bear was once kept at the Tower of London. It was a gift from the king of Norway and used to be taken down to the River Thames every morning to swim.
- The year 46 BCE had 445 days.
- The first hot air balloon flight took place in 1783. On board were a sheep, a rooster, and a duck.
- Forty percent of all the gold that has ever been mined in history has come from South Africa.
- In 1896, Britain went to war with Zanzibar in Africa. The war lasted just 38 minutes!

- The first national lottery ever held in England took place during the reign of Elizabeth I more than 455 years ago.
- During the Second World War, America had the largest army in history.
- Only six people died during the Great Fire of London in 1666...
- ...and when Shakespeare's Globe Theatre burned down in 1613, the only person injured was a man whose trousers caught fire!
- The world's first postage stamp was introduced in England in 1840. Because of its dark color and cheap price, it was called the Penny Black.
- During the Second World War, Germany planned to try to bankrupt England by dropping counterfeit banknotes on London.
- Around one in every 200 men around the world are direct descendants of the famous Mongol leader Genghis Khan.
- In 1952, a London bus was forced to jump the gap in Tower Bridge when the bridge started to open while it was driving across it!
- New York City was once the capital of the USA...
- ...and the town of Colchester was once the capital of the UK.
- The Hundred Years' War lasted 116 years...

- ...while the Thirty Days' War lasted almost a year!
- The Battle of Towton in 1461 was so big that 1% of the entire population of England was killed in it. Numbers: Lancastrians, 30,000-35,000. Royalists, 25,000-30,000.

EXPLORERS

- When Marco Polo encountered rhinoceroses during his travels in Asia, he thought they were unicorns.
- Sir Francis Drake was once the mayor of Plymouth.
- The famous English explorer Richard Burton spoke more than 40 languages.
- Columbus wasn't the first European to visit America. Most historians now think a Viking called Leif Erikson arrived there almost 500 years before him.
- While sailing around America in 1608, the explorer Henry Hudson wrote in his diary that he had seen a mermaid.
- While traveling around the globe in the early 1500s, the explorer Ferdinand Magellan claimed to have discovered a race of giants in South America.
- It was Magellan too who named the Pacific Ocean. Its name literally means "calm" because he thought it looked so peaceful!
- England, Portugal, and France all turned down the chance to pay for Columbus' voyage across the Atlantic Ocean.

- The Dutch explorer Abel Tasman discovered Tasmania—but didn't spot Australia!
- When the Italian explorer Amerigo Vespucci arrived in South America, he saw buildings raised on stilts above the water. Thinking that it reminded him of home, he called the country there Venezuela—which literally means "Little Venice!"
- The mountaineer Sir Edmund Hillary was the first person to climb Mount Everest and he also trekked to both the North and South Poles.
- When the explorer Sir Francis Drake died suddenly during one of his voyages while in Panama in 1596, his crew placed his body in a lead coffin, dressed in a full suit of armor, and dropped it into the sea. Despite many attempts to locate his body, it has never been found.
- According to legend, Sir Francis Drake's dying wish was to have his favorite drum returned to England.
- In 1897, the Australian explorer Frank Hann noticed that some streams in the Australian desert flowed inland, away from the coast. He followed them, expecting to find an enormous lake, but instead found a sandy pool of saltwater—so he called it Lake Disappointment.
- Cadillac cars are named after a French explorer called Antoine de La Mothe Cadillac.

- In 1885, an American explorer named Richard Willoughby claimed to have taken a photograph of an enormous city high above the icy glaciers in Alaska. He sold the photograph to a newspaper in San Francisco for $500—a huge amount of money at the time—before it was discovered that the story was fake. In fact, the photograph was a picture of the English city of Bristol!
- Nobody knows what happened to the explorer Henry Hudson. In 1611, the crew of his ship mutinied and cast him adrift in a rowing boat in the Arctic. He was never seen again.
- When the famous explorer Captain Cook arrived in Hawaii in 1779, some of the locals thought he was a god.
- Sir Francis Drake's ship The Golden Hind was broken apart in 1662, and some of its timbers were used to make a chair. You can still see it in the Bodleian Library in Oxford.

MYTHOLOGY

- Panpipes are named after the Greek god Pan.
- Gods in Ancient Egypt were often depicted as desert animals like lions, falcons, jackals, and ibises.
- Friday is named after the Norse goddess of love, Freya.
- The ancient Sumerian Empire in the Middle East had a specific god, called Ninkasi, who was responsible for beer and brewing, but also fertility, harvest, drunkenness, seduction, and war.
- According to one tale from Norse mythology, the god Loki later gave birth to a grey, eight-legged horse he called Sleipnir.
- ...which the leader of the Norse gods, Odin, is said to have ridden into battle!
- The Egyptian god Re (a.k.a. Ra) was said to sail across the sky in a boat every day, causing the sun to shine...
- ...while nighttime was when Re headed into the Underworld to fight an evil snake god named Apophis. So long as he won that evening's fight, the sun would rise the following morning!

- Medusa wasn't the only snake-headed monster in Greek mythology. She had two sisters, named Stheno and Euryale.
- The two moons of Mars, Phobos and Deimos, are named after the sons of the god of war, Ares, in Greek mythology—while Ares' equivalent in Roman mythology was called Mars!
- The Norse god Odin only had one eye.
- The Greek god of wine, Dionysus, is said to have invented amethyst gemstones by pouring red wine over granite.
- The Egyptian goddess Isis was worshipped far outside Egypt, including in parts of ancient Britain and central Asia.
- In Japanese mythology, two weather gods called Raijin and Fujin are said to have helped defeat the Mongols by raising a storm that held back their invasion of Japan in 1274 and again in 1281.
- As well as being the god of the wilderness and livestock, Pan was also the god of theatre critics.
- The chemical ammonia is named after the Egyptian god Amun...
- ... the Greek goddess Athena gave her name to the capital of Greece, Athens...

- ...and the sports brand Nike is named after the Roman goddess of victory!

ANCIENT EGYPT

- Egyptian hieroglyphs are amongst the oldest writing systems in the world...
- ...and there are over 700 individual hieroglyphic symbols!
- The rulers of Ancient Egypt were called pharaohs. They were named after the enormous palaces in which they lived: the word pharaoh, literally means "great house".
- Some pharaohs used to have their slaves covered in honey to attract flies so that they wouldn't be buzzed by them!
- The Egyptians were expert winemakers...
- ...and are thought to be the first people in history to make bread.
- In fact, they even used moldy bread as medicine!
- Slaves in Ancient Egypt were sometimes paid in garlic.
- Every three years, the pharaoh would have to run around an athletics track to prove they were still fit enough to rule...
- ...and the pharaoh Pepi II lived so long that he had to do it when he was over 80 years old!

- In Ancient Egypt, women usually gave birth while standing up.
- The Egyptian queen Cleopatra spoke nine languages.
- Cleopatra was born in Alexandria, Egypt but she traced her family origins to Macedonian Greece and Ptolemy I Soter, one of Alexander the Great's generals.
- And by the time Cleopatra became queen of Egypt, the pyramids were already 2,500 years old!
- The Egyptians used to wear makeup.
- The pyramids were originally covered in limestone and tipped with gold.
- The Egyptians used to use stone pillows to sleep on.
- In 2019, a loaf of bread was made using yeast found in an Egyptian pot. It was 4,500 years old.
- There are more than 100 pyramids of various shapes & sizes in the Egyptian desert—and there may be more yet to be discovered.
- A lighthouse built at Alexandria in Egypt more than 2,300 years ago was once the tallest building anywhere in the world...
- ...but it collapsed after an earthquake in 1323.

ANCIENT GREECE & ANCIENT ROME

- The months July and August were named after Julius and Augustus Caesar.
- Roman women in Sicily used to wear two-piece bathing suits more than 2,400 years ago!
- The first Olympic athletes in Ancient Greece used to compete naked.
- Rome was supposedly founded by two brothers, Romulus and Remus...
- ...who, according to legend, were raised by a wolf.
- Around one-third of the population of Ancient Greece are thought to have been slaves.
- Historians think that Julius Caesar's nephew Augustus was the richest person ever to have lived.
- Some Greek temples had vending machines that gave out holy water.
- The Romans sometimes flooded their arenas to stage enormous sea battles for the public.
- The Romans used to use their pee as mouthwash!
- Some of the gladiators of Ancient Rome were women...

- ...and most of them were vegetarian!
- The Roman Emperor Caligula wanted to elect his favorite horse, Incitatus, to the Roman counsel...
- ...but he was assassinated before his plan could be carried out!
- In Ancient Greece, the word idiot was used to describe people who had no interest in politics.
- Greek statues might look white in museums today, but they were originally painted in bright colors.
- Some ancient historians believed the Greek island of Santorini is the basis of tales about the lost city of Atlantis!

KINGS AND QUEENS

- Queen Victoria was so well known for bringing fine weather with her on her official royal visits that sunshine was once known as "the Queen's weather."
- Instead of hiring court jesters, a Russian queen named Empress Anna used to have members of her court dress as birds and sit in fake nests to make her laugh.
- The queen of England technically owns all of the dolphins and whales within the British seas.
- King Charles IV of France was so mad that he became convinced he was made of glass and could shatter to pieces at any moment!
- The bones of the famous English king, Richard III were found under a car park in Leicester in 2012.
- Queen Victoria had a parrot that could sing "God Save The Queen."
- When William the Conqueror died in 1087, his body burst as it was being put into his coffin. As priests tried to stuff William into a stone coffin that proved too small for his bulk, they pushed on his abdomen, causing it to burst. Mourners supposedly ran for the door to escape the putrid stench.

- King John of England was the first monarch in history to own a dressing gown.
- In 1520, Henry VIII wrestled the King of France. He lost!
- Queen Elizabeth II has owned more than 30 corgi dogs throughout her life...
- ...the first of which was a dog named Susan that was given to her as a present on her 18th birthday.
- Susan the corgi once bit the official clock-winder at the Royal Lodge at Windsor!
- King Edward III of England once attended a Fancy Dress Christmas banquet dressed as a giant pheasant.
- Mary, I of England had two female jesters.
- Elizabeth I used to have life-size models of people who visited her made out of gingerbread.
- Queen Victoria had a musical dress that played the national anthem when she sat down.
- Louis XIV of France had a gigantic Hall of Mirrors installed at the Palace of Versailles. There are 357 mirrors in it!
- The wedding of Louis XVI and Marie Antoinette of France in 1770 ended when fireworks set fire to the stage. It is said there were over 132 deaths caused by the panic.

- The Queen of England doesn't need a passport...
- ...but she does need money and is said to carry around a little bit of cash in her handbag!

POLITICS AND POLITICIANS

- The British prime minister lives at Number 10, Downing Street, in London. Despite the address, the house is actually several houses knocked into one.
- The grounds of the White House cover 18 acres.
- US President Richard Nixon was a keen musician and played the piano, violin, accordion, clarinet, and saxophone.
- President Lyndon Johnson used to give interviews in his bathtub.
- The American president Zachary Taylor died after eating too many cherries. At the time, little suspicion clouded Taylor's death. Doctors chalked it up to *cholera morbus* after the president consumed cherries and iced milk during a Fourth of July celebration.
- After President Andrew Jackson died, his pet parrot was brought to his funeral...
- ...but it had to be removed from the church because it kept swearing!
- Abraham Lincoln was a wrestler. Defeated only once in approximately 300 matches.
- President James Buchanan kept a pet eagle.

- It takes 570 gallons of paint to repaint the White House.
- President Chester A Arthur sold 20 wagonloads of furniture from the White House when he moved into it because he thought it was too crowded.
- President Harry Truman called the White House "the finest prison in the world."
- President James Garfield could write with his left and right hand at the same time...
- ...and supposedly could write in different languages simultaneously!
- The first US president, George Washington, never lived at the White House.
- After he had been president, George Washington made whiskey for a living.
- Before he became US president, Gerald Ford worked as a male model...
- ...and once appeared on the cover of *Cosmopolitan* magazine.
- President Calvin Coolidge had a pet hippo called William Johnson Hippopotamus.
- In 1987, the British prime minister Margaret Thatcher appeared on a kid's television show called *Saturday Superstore* and gave her opinion on the latest pop charts.

- President John Quincy Adams used to like swimming naked in the river beside the White House.
- There are 35 bathrooms in the White House.

STUPENDOUS SCIENCE

INVENTIONS AND INVENTORS

- One of the main ingredients in glass is sand.
- The tin can opener was invented 48 years after the tin can.
- The fuel used to send astronauts into space was invented in 1926. The man who invented it, Robert H. Goddard, was originally made fun of when he said it was powerful enough to send people to the Moon!
- Bubble Wrap was invented by accident by two inventors trying to make 3D wallpaper...
- ...while Play-Doh was originally invented as a substance to clean dirty marks off the wallpaper.
- Slinky springs were invented when a big metal spring actually fell off a shelf and uncoiled its way to the ground.
- The dentist's chair was invented in France in the 1700s. Before then, most dental surgeries were conducted with the patient lying on the floor!
- The inventor of the telephone, Alexander Graham Bell, thought that people should say "ahoy" when they answer it, not "hello".
- Laser technology stands for "light amplification by stimulated emission of radiation"...

- ...while a diver's scuba gear stands for "self-contained underwater breathing apparatus!"
- The payphone was invented in 1889. Within ten years, there were more than 80,000 of them in America.
- One of the most successful inventors at the Nintendo game company began as the office caretaker.
- In 1868, a new motorized carriage was invented that was pulled by a steam-powered robotic man.
- Corn Flakes were invented by mistake when a tray of wheat was overcooked by their inventor, Will Kellogg.
- French fries were actually invented in Belgium.
- Thomas Edison supposedly claimed that a successful inventor needed two things: "a good imagination and a pile of junk."
- Diesel engines are named after a man called Rudolph Diesel.
- One of the very first bicycles was called the dandy-horse.
- Mechanical firelighters were invented before matches.
- Cowboy hats are properly called Stetson hats. They're named after their inventor—an American hatmaker named John B. Stetson.

- One of the earliest models of a mechanical typewriter was called the "literary piano".
- The modern fork was invented in Italy in the 11th century...
- ...but they were originally unpopular because people saw them as unnecessary alternatives to using your fingers!
- The sticking fabric Velcro was invented by a Swiss scientist named George de Mestral, who based his design on sticky grass seeds.
- The first recorded electric car was developed in 1891.
- Thomas Edison proposed to his wife in Morse Code.
- Plastic was invented accidentally by a Belgian chemist named Leo Baekeland. The first commercial plastic was called Bakelite in his honor!

PHYSICS AND CHEMISTRY

- Electricity moves at about nine-tenths the speed of light—about 165,000 miles a second!
- The hardest material in the world is a diamond...
- ...and at high temperatures, diamonds don't burn—they vaporize!
- Birds can sit on powerlines and not be electrocuted because they don't complete a circuit. If they were to touch two powerlines at the same time, they would be killed!
- Gravity not only holds you to the ground—but it also holds the Moon alongside the Earth!
- Sound produces heat.
- 98% of everything in the universe is made of hydrogen and helium.
- The "crack" of a whip is actually a mini sonic boom—an explosive sound wave, caused by the motion of the whip breaking the sound barrier!
- Glass is actually a liquid. That's why old windows are often thicker at the bottom than at the top—the glass very slowly flows downward over time, like water!
- The periodic table is a list of all the basic chemicals used in science. The scientist who

invented it, Dmitri Mendeleev, now has an element named after him: mendelevium.

- The shortest named chemical element on the periodic table is tin.
- Light slows down when it passes through water.
- The electricity supply in a standard home is around 120 volts of power...
- ...but a single strike of lightning is around 300 million volts and produces enough energy to burn off a quarter of a billion calories!
- 99% of an atom is just empty space—and because atoms make up everything in the universe, 99% of everything is empty!
- If you were to travel at the speed of light, time would stop.
- The faster you go, the heavier you become.
- Sound travels through solid matter faster than it does through the air.

DISCOVERIES

- Human beings are thought to have discovered fire more than 1 million years ago. The oldest unequivocal evidence, found at Israel's Qesem Cave, dates back 300,000 to 400,000 years, associating the earliest control of fire with Homo sapiens and Neanderthals. Now, however, an international team of archaeologists has unearthed what appear to be traces of campfires that flickered 1 million years ago.
- We have been using numbers and measurements for more than 5,000 years...
- ...while algebra was developed in an ancient region called Babylonia 4,000 years ago!
- The Ancient Greeks are known to have discovered that the Earth is round more than 2,500 years ago.
- The medicine penicillin was discovered accidentally when a glass dish was left to go moldy on the windowsill of a laboratory in London.
- The ability to cook using microwaves was discovered by accident too in the 1940s, when a chocolate bar was found to have been melted by military radar equipment!

- A chemical called nitrous oxide is better known as a laughing gas because it causes people to laugh uncontrollably. In the 1800s, it was discovered that it also stops people from feeling pain—and so the use of gas in medical procedures was invented!
- People started making buildings out of bricks 9,000 years ago. Bricks date back to 7000 BC, which makes them one of the oldest known building materials.
- One of the earliest recorded toys is the kite. The first kites were used in China around 2,500 years ago.
- Quinine is the name of a medicine used to treat malaria—a dangerous disease spread by mosquitos. According to legend, the medicine was discovered when a man suffering from malaria drank water from a pool beneath a tree containing quinine in the Amazon rainforest and survived!
- Medical x-rays were discovered by a scientist named Wilhelm Roentgen, who found that he could see his bones on a glowing screen whenever an electrical tube was turned on in his laboratory!

MATHEMATICS AND NUMBERS

- The number four has four letters. It's the only English number spelled with the same number of letters as it describes.
- 12,345,679 multiplied by the missing number eight is 98,765,432.
- A number one followed by 100 zeroes is called a googol...
- ...while a one followed by a googol of zeroes is called a googolplex!
- A triangle with sides 3, 4, and 5 centimeters long will have an area of 6 square centimeters!
- The Romans used the letters I, V, X, L, C, and M for their numbers...
- ...but they had no numeral to represent zero.
- A hundred is 100—but a long-hundred is 120.
- A number that can only be divided equally by itself and one is called a prime number. The only even prime number is two.
- All multiples of ten end in zero.
- 111,111,111 × 111,111,111 = 12,345,678,987,654,321.
- No matter how high you count, every number from 89 onward has the letter N in its name.

- The digits that make all numbers that can be divided equally by three add up to multiples of three. So, 12 is 1 + 2 — and 1 + 2 makes 3!
- The fraction 1/7 written out as a decimal is 0.142857142857142857... The sequence of numbers "123857" would repeat on and on forever!
- When five dots or shapes are arranged in a square, with the fifth dot in the middle—like the five on a die—the pattern it makes is called a quincunx.
- The numbers we use today were developed in central and western Asia more than 1,000 years ago.
- Numbers on opposite sides of a six-faced die always add up to seven.
- 10 × 9 × 8 × 7 × 6 × 5 × 4 × 3 × 2 × 1 = 3,628,800...
- ...which is exactly the number of seconds in six weeks!
- Because the number five is pronounced "ha" in some southeast Asian languages, 555 is used to represent laughter in text messages.
- Forty is the only number whose letters are spelled in alphabetical order—F, O, R, T, Y.
- A shape with 99 sides would be called an enneacontakaienneagon.

- A Fibonacci sequence is a string of numbers in which each entry is the preceding two numbers added together: 0, 1, 1, 2, 3, 5, 8, 13, 21...
- The number above the line in a fraction is called the numerator. The number below is called the denominator. The line that separates them is called the vinculum.
- If the numerator is a bigger number than the denominator, then the fraction is called improper, like 5/4. In a proper fraction, the numerator is lower than the denominator, like 1/2.

OUR BRILLIANT BODIES

THE HUMAN BODY

- The tongue is the only muscle in the human body that is not attached at both ends.
- Your body produces around 25 million new cells every second...
- ...around 17 million of which are red blood cells.
- On average, your hair will grow around 6 inches every year.
- The funny bone isn't actually a bone—it's a nerve!
- Your lips are red because your skin is thinnest around the mouth, making the blood vessels below the skin more visible.
- While the inside of your hand is called the palm, the outside or back of the hand is properly called the opisthenar.
- Your eyes blink around 20 times every minute.
- Men produce more sweat than women, but women have more sweat glands than men.
- There are around 30 million red blood cells in a single teaspoon of blood.
- There are around 8,000 taste buds on your tongue that help you to taste everything you eat. *The* average human tongue has between

2000 and 8000 taste buds, but it can vary between 500 and 20,000.

- Saliva helps start to break down food inside your mouth even before you've swallowed it.
- The hard white coating of your teeth is called enamel. It is the hardest substance in the entire body—even harder than bone!
- You are taller in the morning than in the evening.
- The thighbone is the longest bone in the body.
- There is naturally a tiny amount of gold in your blood.
- Our brains use up around one-fifth of our body's oxygen supply...
- ...despite only taking up around 2% of our entire body weight!
- Around two-thirds of the entire human body is water.
- The cornea is the clear covering of the front of the eye. Because it has to be perfectly clear...
- ...it is the only part of the body without its own blood supply.
- Your skin is covered in millions of microscopic holes called pores...

- ...which cover every part of the body except the palms of your hands and the soles of your feet.
- The inside of our intestines isn't smooth but covered in lots of finger-like lobes called villi. If they were all smoothed out, our intestines could cover an area the size of a tennis court!
- On average, a person's heart beats around 3 billion times in their entire life.
- The top part of the stomach is called the fundus—which is the Latin word for "bottom"!
- You'll breathe around 17,000 times a day...
- ...and depending on your size, will process more than 2,300 gallons of air!
- There are around 60,000 miles of blood vessels in your body!
- On average, women's hearts beat faster than men's hearts.
- Like your tongue, your pancreas has cells in it that can taste things. You don't know they do that, however, because, unlike your tongue, they don't relay their signals back to your brain.
- There are three tiny bones in the ear called the hammer, the stirrup, and the anvil. Without them, we wouldn't be able to hear!

- Your lungs contain cells called alveoli that help us breathe. On average, a person's lungs will contain around 600 million of them.
- Your eyes contain two types of cells, called rods and cones, which help us to see. Cones help us see in color and detail—but there are around 20 times more rods than cones!
- Babies have more bones than adults. As they grow older, some smaller bones fuse together...
- ...until an adult has a total of 206.
- Although some people have more bones—some people grow an extra pair of ribs!
- By weight, the skin is the largest organ in our body.
- The hyoid bone is a bone in the throat that helps to support the tongue. It is the only bone in the body not attached to any other.
- You have more bones in your hands and feet than in the rest of your body added together!
- The acid in your stomach is stronger than vinegar and can even break down bone and teeth.
- It is impossible to sneeze with your eyes open.

ASTOUNDING ANIMALS

MAMMALS

- Bats are the only mammals that are capable of flying...
- ...though some mammals have membranes between their legs that allow them to glide.
- Cheetahs are the fast of all land mammals. They can run at speeds of around 75- 80 mph!
- An adult koala can eat almost 2.2 lbs. of eucalyptus leaves in a single day.
- Horses are distant relatives of rhinoceroses.
- Polar bears have black skin.
- When a duck-billed platypus was first displayed in England, people thought it was a joke.
- As well as being the largest mammal, the blue whale is the largest creature that has ever lived.
- Giraffes have the same number of bones in their necks as we do.
- Camel humps are made of fat and the humps do not store water.
- A cross between a male tiger and a female lion is called a liger...
- ...while a cross between a male lion and a female tiger is called a tigon.

- A giraffe's pattern of blotches is as unique as our fingerprints—and so are zebra stripes, tiger stripes, and the indentations on a dog's nose!
- Elephants have the biggest ears in the animal kingdom.
- Cats don't have collarbones.
- Dalmatian dogs are born completely white and only develop their famous black spots as they grow older.
- Horses can't breathe through their mouths.
- Humans are the only primate that cannot breathe and swallow at the same time...
- ...but the mechanism that stops us from doing that is also what allows us to speak!
- A mouse will eat 20 times a day.
- Beluga whales have such complicated calls that they are known as the "canaries of the sea!"
- The closest living relative to the elephant is a tiny gopher-like mammal called a rock hyrax.
- Some animals, like rabbits and horses, have their eyes so far round on the sides of their heads that they can see almost everything around them.

- Otters have the densest fur of any animal. On some parts of their body, there are 1 million hairs in a single inch of skin!
- Some species of bats live for more than 40 years.
- A camel can drink 26 gallons of water in ten minutes.
- Rhino horns are made of keratin—the same substance from which your hair and fingernails are made!
- A rabbit's tail is called a scut.
- A hippo's skin is so thick that they are almost bulletproof...
- ...and so are armadillo shells!
- As well as chimps and gorillas, some of the most intelligent mammals in the world include hyenas, raccoons, and pigs.
- In fact, raccoons are smart enough to pick locks.
- Koalas sleep for around 20 hours every day.
- The Javan rhinoceros is the rarest land mammal in the world. There are thought to be fewer than 67 individuals in the wild.
- Jaguars have the strongest bite of any other mammal in the animal kingdom.

- Pound for pound, leopards are the strongest of the big cats and can haul animals they have killed more than 50 ft into a tree so that other animals don't steal from them!
- There are 40,000 muscles in an elephant's trunk.
- Kangaroos can't walk backwards, and muscular legs make it easy for them to move forward effectively but those appendages stop them from going in reverse.
- Bears can run as fast as horses.
- A hedgehog has around 6,000 quills (spines).
- While most animals hibernate only for the winter, some species of dormice sleep for 11 months of the year!
- Wolverines are large bear-like mammals that live in the Arctic. Despite being known for their ferociousness, they belong to the same family of animals as badgers!
- Tigers have striped skin as well as fur.
- Platypus mothers feed their young by sweating milk through their skin. Their milk oozes out of mammary gland ducts and collects in grooves on their skin—where the nursing babies lap it up or suck it from tufts of fur.

- The longest-lived mammal is the bowhead whale. Scientists believe they can live for more than 200 years!

BIRDS

- All birds have feathers.
- A group of owls is called a parliament…
- …while a group of flamingos is called a flamboyance…
- …and a flock of crows is called a murder!
- There are more than 11,000 species of birds in the world.
- Birds are the closest living family of animals to dinosaurs.
- Female blackbirds are brown, not black.
- Toucans are known to feed on other birds' eggs and for a long time were known as egg-suckers!
- Pelicans can hold up to 3 gallons of water in their pouchy beaks.
- A single woodpecker can strike its head against a tree 12,000 times in a day.
- Flamingos feed while holding their heads upside down.
- The Arctic Tern is a small seabird that has the longest migration of any bird in the world. Every summer, they fly 11,000 miles from one pole to the other!

- A bird called the Hooded Pitohui that lives in New Guinea has a toxin in its skin and feathers that make it the only poisonous bird in the world!
- Owls' eyes aren't round—they're cylindrical. For this reason, an owl cannot "roll" or move its eyes—that is, it can only look straight ahead!
- All penguins are found in the southern hemisphere...
- ...but not all of them are in the Antarctic! There are penguins in Australia, Africa, and South America.
- There are even penguins in the Galapagos Islands on the equator!
- Hummingbirds are to be the only birds that can fly backwards.
- Some birds that have to fly long distances at a time, like swifts and albatrosses, can sleep in the air.
- There are enough chickens in the world to give four of them to everyone on Earth.
- Ostriches can run at speeds of around 45 mph with a top speed of 60 miles per hour for short bursts....
- ...and can cover around 16 ft in a single stride!
- Kiwis are the smallest flightless birds in the world...

- ...but lay the biggest eggs compared to the size of their bodies of all birds! A single egg can weigh around one-quarter of an adult bird's body weight. That's like a human mother giving birth to a four-year-old child!
- Owls swallow their prey whole, then throw up anything they can't digest, like bones and fur!
- Ostriches have three stomachs...
- ...and swallow stones to help grind up their food.
- The Lammergeier is an enormous vulture that has such strong acid in its stomach it can eat bones and is traditionally revered as the sacred bird of Tibet.
- Birds can fly because—unlike mammals—their bones are hollow.
- A male peacock has more than 100 eye-shaped markings on his tail feathers.
- Puffins nest underground. They often lay their eggs in rabbit burrows.
- Swans mate for life and will continue to have chicks with the same partner for their entire lives.
- Hummingbirds' hearts beat more than 600 times a minute.
- Owls have one ear higher than the other.

- The fleshy wattles that hang over a turkey's beak is called a snood.

REPTILES AND AMPHIBIANS

- Reptiles do not sweat...
- ...and all reptiles have scales!
- Snakes smell with their tongues.
- Crocodiles can hold their breath underwater for more than an hour.
- Geckos' feet are so sticky they can hang upside down from the ceiling!
- The Anaconda is the biggest snake in the world. They can grow to around 220 lbs—and some individuals have been said to be nearly 30 ft long!
- Sea turtles will return to the beach on which they were born to lay their own eggs.
- Reptiles are some of the longest-living animals in the world. A tortoise named Jonathan that lives on a reserve in the Seychelles islands was born in 1832 and is still alive today!
- Crocodiles and alligators have no lips...
- ...and they cannot stick their tongues out!
- Lizards can shed their own tails to escape from a predator. The tail will eventually grow back.
- Slow worms are actually legless lizards, not worms or snakes.

- A chameleon's two eyes can look in different directions at the same time.
- To escape predators, American horned lizards can squirt blood from their eyes!
- A Hundred-Pacer is a species of snake that is so venomous that it is believed that its prey can only move 100 steps away from it after they have been bitten before dying!
- Sidewinder snakes can slither at 18 mph.
- A group of crocodiles is called a bask.
- Crocodiles have the strongest bite of any creature in the world.
- Reptiles are ectothermic—meaning they cannot produce their own body heat. This causes a problem in wintry weather, and lizards sometimes fall out of trees on cold nights!
- Each of the hard plates in a tortoise's shell is called a scute.
- Crocodiles sit with their mouths open to cool down.
- Someone, who studies reptiles and amphibians, is called a herpetologist.
- The Asian Saw-Scaled Viper is thought to be responsible for up to 90% of all snake-bite-related deaths per year in Asia.

- In 1919, a crocodile suddenly appeared on the island nation of Fiji in the south Pacific. Because crocodiles are not native to Fiji, it was thought that it must have swum 600 miles from the nearest population of crocodiles in another group of islands.
- Crocodiles have so many nerves in their skin that their faces are ten times more sensitive than your fingertips.
- Some species of frogs and toads use pressure from their eyeballs to help swallow their food.
- North American Wood Frogs don't just hibernate during winter—wood frogs freeze up to 60 percent of their bodies during the long and extremely cold Alaskan winters, they freeze themselves then defrost in the spring!
- A young newt is called an eft...
- ...while a young toad is called a toadlet.
- The flat-headed frog has no lungs and breathes through its skin instead!
- An adult crocodile will go through around 4,000 teeth in its lifetime.
- On land, crocodiles can run at up to 12 mph. When running on their belly, crocodiles reach an average speed of around 7.4 mph.

UNDER THE SEA

- Sharks have existed on Earth longer than trees have.
- Not all fish have scales.
- Female lobsters are called chickens.
- Sharks don't have bones.
- Parrotfish sleep in bubbles.
- Some species of eel leave the rivers of Europe in Fall and swim across the Atlantic Ocean to breed—a journey of more than 3,000 miles!
- Deep sea hagfish produce slime by mixing mucus from their skin with the surrounding water. In less than a minute, typically, a hagfish will release less than a teaspoon of gunk from the 100 or so slime glands that line its flanks. And in less than half a second, that little amount will expand by 10,000 times—enough to fill a sizable bucket.
- Some female swordfish lay nearly 30 million eggs...
- ...while a single female sunfish can lay nearly ten times that many in a year!
- The Bombay Duck is actually a fish, not a duck.
- Electric eels can produce enough electricity to kill a horse. Early explorers described

electric eel shocks knocking down horses which subsequently drowned. A large shock could cause respiratory paralysis and heart failure in humans.

- Flying fish leap out of the water and travel through the air by as much as 164 ft or longer...
- ...but technically, despite their name, they glide, not fly.
- Sharks would drown if they stopped swimming...
- ...and cannot swim backwards, either.
- Starfish and jellyfish aren't fish. Both lack brains or skeletons, and neither are fish at all. They are marine animals, meaning they live in the saltwater of the ocean.
- Some jellyfish have tentacles that are 300 ft long!
- The Sailfish is said to be the fastest fish in the sea. It can swim at speeds of almost 70 mph!
- Mudskipper fish can store a portable water supply in their gills and haul themselves onto land to live out of water for up to two days!
- Some fish, such as salmon, can swim up waterfalls to reach their breeding grounds inland.
- A baby eel is called an elver.

- Seahorses are the only fish that swim upright.
- Some species of tuna fish can live for up to 50 years and grow to more than 6 ft in length.
- Catfish have four times more taste buds on their tongues than we do.
- The Pacific Stonefish is the most venomous fish in the world...
- ...which is a problem because they can live out of the water on beaches for up to 24 hours!

INSECTS AND CREEPY-CRAWLIES

- As well as eight legs, spiders have eight eyes.
- A single honeybee can visit up to 100 flowers in just one trip out of the hive...
- ...and can pollinate anywhere from 3,000 to 5,000 flowers in a single day!
- Snails are deaf.
- Velvet ants are actually wasps. Female velvet ants are wingless.
- Antarctica is the only continent in the world that is not home to spiders.
- Ants can carry up to 50 times their own body weight. That's like an average adult man carrying a family car on both shoulders!
- Horseflies can fly at 90 mph.
- Insects like grasshoppers make their chirruping sound by rubbing their legs together...
- ...which is a process called stridulation.
- Butterflies taste things with their feet.
- There are four times more species of insects on Earth than all the other species of living creatures added together.

- Ants are the longest-lived of all insects. The queens of some ant species can live for more than 20 years!
- Some species of tarantulas can fire their rough, spiny hairs out of their bodies to deter predators.
- A bee will travel up to 6 miles in search of nectar.
- It was once believed that dancing could cure the pain of a tarantula bite. The dance was called the "tarantella".
- By weight, spider silk is stronger than steel.
- Mosquitos are attracted to smelly feet.
- In some countries, snail slime is used as a skin cream and is said to have anti-ageing properties.
- The world's largest butterfly is Queen Alexandra's Birdwing. Its wings are nearly 1 ft wide!
- A bee has four wings, not two...
- ...and beats them nearly 200 times a second!
- According to folklore, keeping conkers around your home is meant to stop spiders from creeping inside. Chestnuts and conkers are quite different from each other, especially in the fact that chestnuts are edible, and conkers are not. That said, the two nuts are often

confused for each other, as they both have the same reddish-brown color and conkers are often referred to as horse chestnuts.

- African cicadas are the loudest insects in the world. They can produce noises as loud as a crying baby.
- A grasshopper's ears are on its belly.
- Some butterflies' wings are completely transparent and look like little glass windows.

DINOSAURS AND EXTINCT ANIMALS

- Of all the animals that have ever lived on Earth, 99% are now extinct.
- The word dinosaur literally means "monstrous lizard".
- Tyrannosaurus Rex is thought to have been the largest meat-eating creature ever to have lived...
- ...though some dinosaur experts think it wasn't a hunter and might have just fed on smaller dinosaurs that were already dead!
- A brachiosaurus' neck was around 30 ft long!
- Velociraptor literally means "swift thief", which is derived from the Latin words "velox" (swift) and "raptor" (robber or plunderer)
- ...while stegosaurus literally means "roofed lizard!"
- A triceratops' skull weighed one-third of its entire body weight.
- The very first dinosaurs appeared around 230 million years ago.
- The plates on a stegosaurus' back were covered in blood vessels and so could probably

be flushed and turned a bright red color—just like a person's blushing cheeks!

- Although most scientists believe that a meteor strike was to blame, no one knows for sure why the dinosaurs died out.
- Argentinosaurus was the largest dinosaur that ever lived. A fully grown adult would have stood around 130 ft long and weighed more than 100 tons! Argentinosaurus is a genus of giant sauropod dinosaurs that lived during the Late Cretaceous period in what is now Argentina.
- Despite a stegosaurus standing around 15 ft long and weighing more than 2 tons, its brain was only around the size of a walnut!
- Micropachycephalosaurus is the longest recorded dinosaur name. It has 23 letters!
- In 2020, a tiny dinosaur skull was found encased in amber in the jungle of southeast Asia. It is thought to have belonged to the smallest dinosaur that ever lived—which likely weighed less than 6 ounces!
- The moa was a gigantic flightless bird that once roamed the grasslands of New Zealand. Similar to other large birds, like ostriches and emus, it was 12 ft tall!
- Domestic cats are thought to have led to more than 60 different creatures going extinct

since humans first started keeping them as pets.

- In the late 1800s, a pet cat named Tibbles which was kept by the lighthouse keeper on Stephens Island, off the coast of New Zealand killed all the Wrens on the island. So, the Stephens Island Wren—a bird found nowhere else in the world—became extinct because of a single pet cat!
- The dodo bird was discovered in 1598 on the island of Mauritius in the Indian Ocean. They were hunted to extinction within 65 years and the last live bird was spotted on the island in 1662.
- Ancient cave paintings in France show cave people living alongside huge cow-like animals called aurochs. The creatures roamed the forests of Europe for thousands of years before they were hunted to extinction in 1627.
- The world's largest meat-eating marsupial was the thylacine or Tasmanian Tiger. About the size of a fox or a small wolf, the thylacine was seen as a threat to livestock and hunted for its fur. The last surviving animal died in a zoo in 1936.
- The last surviving animal of its species is called an endling.

FANTASTIC FOOD

FANTASTIC FOOD

- Tomato ketchup was originally a bitter fish sauce and was used in some East Asia countries as a medicine.
- The fresher an egg is, the higher it will float when you place it in water...
- ...so bad eggs tend to sink!
- The sandwich is named after an English nobleman called John Montagu, the Earl of Sandwich.
- The cardboard loop that is sometimes placed around hot coffee cups to make them easier to hold is called a zarf.
- There are more than 300 different pasta shapes.
- Cucumbers are 96% water.
- Bananas are faintly radioactive. Bananas glow blue under black lights. The closer to being ripe, the brighter the banana glows.
- The world's first chewing gum factory opened in Portland, Maine, in the 1850s. Some of the first chewing gums, made of birch tar and other natural substances, have been preserved for thousands of years, including a 5,700-year-old piece of Stone Age gum unearthed in Denmark.

- Traditionally, if a scone has been made correctly, it shouldn't need to be cut—you should be able to break it down the middle into two matching halves!
- The world's oldest loaf of bread was found in the desert of Jordan in the Middle East in 2018. It was found to be 14,400 years old!
- In 2012, five Italian chefs produced the world's largest pizza. It was more than 13,500 sq ft—or more than six times the size of a tennis court!
- Half the world's orange juice comes from Brazil.
- Carrots aren't naturally orange. They were originally purple but have been crossbred over centuries to change them into brighter, sweeter vegetables!
- Potato crisps are worse for your teeth than candy.
- Breakfast is so-called because it was once the meal that "broke" the "fast" of the previous evening.
- You can eat gold.
- The earliest known lasagna recipe was published almost 700 years ago.
- It takes around 400 cocoa beans to make a single bar of chocolate.

- Cheese and tomato pizzas are named Margherita pizzas after Queen Margherita of Savoy, who was the Queen of Italy from 1878–1900.
- Biscuits and crackers have holes in them to stop them from rising too much when they are baked.
- In 2013, engineers in England developed a car that could run on coffee.
- Pineapples aren't from pine trees and are unrelated to apples.
- American chefs in the 1800s invented a simple cake called a "one-two-three-four" that contained one cup of butter, two cups of sugar, three cups of flour, and four eggs.
- Eating too many carrots can make your skin go orange...
- ...as can drinking too much orange juice!
- While the yellow part of an egg is called the yolk, the white part is called the albumen.
- In 2014, a man in Saudi Arabia made a teabag that weighed 550 lbs!
- The process of producing bread is called panification.
- Because there is so much carbon in peanut butter, scientists could use enormous pressure to turn it into diamonds!

- Despite the popularity of chicken and beef, the world's most consumed meat is goat.
- A single strand of spaghetti is called a spaghetto.
- Because it doesn't contain any cocoa, technically white chocolate isn't actually chocolate.
- Vodka literally means "little water".
- Sweetcorn is really a type of grass.
- Every year, McDonald's sells around 2.5 billion hamburgers!
- Honey never goes bad or moldy. In fact, honey that has been found in the pyramids of Ancient Egypt is still good to eat!
- Chilis are ranked on a scale called the Scoville scale, with the hottest tasting chilis at the top. A pepper only scores around 100 units on the Scoville scale—but the world's hottest chili peppers score more than 3 million!
- People in Finland drink more coffee per person than in any other country.
- Potatoes were the first food ever grown in space.
- World Pasta Day is celebrated on October 25.
- The spice saffron is so rare that it is more expensive to buy than gold.

- Stargazy pie is a traditional Cornish delicacy that has fish heads poking out the top of it!
- Fortune cookies come from San Francisco, USA, not China.
- Strawberries aren't berries...
- ...but bananas are!
- In 2010, chefs in Japan produced a single strand of pasta that was more than 12,000 ft long.

AWESOME ART & ARTISTS

ART AND ARTISTS

- In 2016, a famous Leonardo da Vinci painting was sold at auction in New York for $450.3 million—making it the most expensive painting in the world!
- When he was a baby, the famous Spanish artist Pablo Picasso's first word was the Spanish word for "pencil".
- In 1917, the French artist Marcel Duchamp put a sculpture called *Fountain* on display in a museum in New York. The sculpture was just a urinal!
- Vincent Van Gogh only sold one painting in his lifetime.
- Painting and sculpture were once contested at the Olympic Games.
- "Da Vinci" was not Leonardo da Vinci's surname. In fact, it just means "from Vinci"—the name of the town in Italy where he was born. His full name was 'Leonardo di ser Piero da Vinci'.
- The French artist Paul Gauguin helped to build the Panama Canal.
- Picasso produced nearly 150,000 artworks in his lifetime.
- By the time he died in 1519, Leonardo da Vinci had not finished the Mona Lisa...

- ...and not only that, but no one knows for sure who the Lisa in the portrait actually is!
- Despite being one of the most famous artists in history, Claude Monet was told by his father to abandon his dreams of becoming a painter and become a vegetable seller instead!
- The artist Salvador Dali was terrified of grasshoppers.
- When the Mona Lisa was stolen in 1911, Pablo Picasso was one of the main suspects...
- ...and the Mona Lisa is now so valuable that it is kept behind bulletproof glass!
- The French artist Henri Matisse's painting *Le Bateau* was once hung upside down at a gallery in New York. Nobody noticed for forty-seven days!

MUSIC

- The composer JS Bach wrote an opera about how much he liked coffee.
- By the time of his last public performance, Beethoven was so deaf that he had to be turned around to see the audience clapping him.
- Among the treatments doctors prescribed to try to cure Beethoven's deafness was taking baths in river water and pouring warm honey into his ears.
- Mozart kept a pet starling.
- The carol "Jingle Bells" was originally written for Thanksgiving, not Christmas...
- ...It was also one of the first songs ever sung in space.
- Plants grow faster when they're played music...
- ...and dairy cows produce more milk!
- The third largest crater on the planet Mercury is named after Beethoven.
- The song "Happy Birthday" earns its owners around $5,000 in royalties every day.
- When they listen to music, some people's heartbeats synchronize to its beat.

- On average, 40,000 new tracks are added to the Spotify streaming service every day.
- Karaoke means "empty orchestra" in Japanese.
- The American composer John Cage wrote a piece of music called 4'33". It is nothing except 4 minutes and 33 seconds of absolute silence.

POP AND ROCK

- The average pop song lasts 3 minutes and 42 seconds.
- Elvis Presley's famous black hair was fake. His hair was naturally blonde, and he dyed it black.
- Elvis has had nearly 150 songs listed on the American music charts.
- The Beatles have sold more records than any other music act in history.
- The pop star Elton John started playing the piano when he was four years old...
- ...while the singer Tori Amos started playing the piano when she was only two!
- The drummer in the rock band Def Leppard only had one arm.
- The pop band ABBA is named after its members: Agnetha (A), Björn (B), Benny (B), and Anni-Frid (A).
- The famous musician Bob Marley was buried with one of his guitars.
- Mariah Carey reportedly has a vocal range covering more than five octaves.
- Adele and Jessie J went to school together.

- Rock band Blondie was originally called Angel and the Snake...
- ...while pop group Maroon 5 was originally named Kara's Flowers.
- In 2013, the rock band Metallica became the first act in history to perform a concert on all seven continents when they performed in Antarctica!
- The song "Despacito" by Luis Fonsi and Justin Bieber has been watched more than 7.5 billion times on YouTube—that's almost more than the number of people in the whole world...
- ...while the famous "Baby Shark" children's music video is now the first video in YouTube's history to be watched more than 10 billion times!
- In 2017, Katy Perry became the first person to get 100 million Twitter followers.
- In November 2021, Taylor Swift's "All Too Well" became the longest song ever to reach Number 1 in America. At 10 minutes, 13 seconds, it beat the previous record holder—Don McLean's "American Pie"—by 1 minute and 36 seconds.

MUSICAL INSTRUMENTS

- The piano was invented in 1720.
- After he first heard someone play the guitar, Beethoven said it was like "a miniature orchestra."
- The world's oldest musical instrument is a flute made from bone that was discovered in 2006. It is thought to be 40,000 years old.
- More than 70 individual pieces of wood are joined together to make a violin.
- There are 88 keys on a standard piano.
- The first musical instruments played in space were a harmonica and a bell. It was smuggled on board NASA's Gemini 6 spacecraft by one of the astronauts in 1965.
- The world's loudest musical instrument is a pipe organ found in Boardwalk Hall Auditorium in Atlantic City, USA. It has more than 1,000 keys, and 33,000 pipes, and produces notes louder than the whistle on a steam train!
- A standard tuba contains 16 ft of coiled brass tubing.
- Bagpipes were invented in Ancient Egypt and were popular with the Romans who took them to ancient Britannia.

- The octobass is an enormous stringed instrument that looks like a giant cello but stands almost 11 ft tall. It is so large that to play it a musician has to stand on a chair!
- There is a cave in Virginia, USA, where musicians can play the rock formations using a keyboard. The keys are attached to mallets that strike the stalactites and stalagmites in the cave.
- A flugelhorn is a small brass instrument, resembling a trumpet. A cross between a flugelhorn and a tuba is called a fluba!
- A person who makes violin bows is called an archetier...
- ...while a person who makes violins and other stringed instruments is called a luthier.
- There are more than 12,000 individual parts in a standard piano.

THE MOVIES

- Movie trailers are so called because they were originally shown "trailing" after the main movie.
- *The Lord of the Rings* trilogy of movies cost $281 million...
- ...but earned almost $3 billion!
- In *The Wizard of Oz*, the oil used to lubricate the Tin Man's joints was actually chocolate syrup.
- The computer-animated movie *Toy Story 2* was almost accidentally deleted before it was complete when the computers at Pixar developed a fault.
- In the entire history of the Oscars, only one winning movie has ever been disqualified: in 1968, a documentary called *The Young Americans* had the Oscar taken from it when it emerged that it had been released a year earlier than the rules allowed!
- In the famous gangster movie, *The Godfather*, the main character is often seen holding a pet cat. In fact, the cat was a stray and the actor, Marlon Brando, had only found it that morning wandering around the set and decided to keep hold of it during filming!

- The historical scenes in the movie *Titanic* last precisely as long on screen as it took the ship to sink.
- The animated ogre Shrek wasn't originally meant to have a Scottish accent. The film had almost been completed when the decision to change it was made.
- *The Lion King* is based on Shakespeare's play *Hamlet*.
- Despite appearances, the villain Ursula in Disney's *The Little Mermaid* isn't an octopus: she only has six tentacles, because the filmmakers thought animating eight would be too difficult!
- In early versions of the movie *Tangled*, Pascal the chameleon was originally a squirrel.
- The idea behind Disney's *Frozen* was originally pitched 70 years before the movie was made.
- In the original *Jurassic Park* movie, the dinosaurs are only on screen for around 15 minutes.
- The character Luke Skywalker in *Star Wars* was originally due to be called Luke Skykiller...
- ...while Yoda was originally called Buffy!
- And swashbuckling hero Indiana Jones was originally going to be called Indiana Smith!

ACTORS AND ACTRESSES

- The 1920s Hollywood actress Mary Pickford was known around the world as "America's Sweetheart"—even though she was born in Canada!
- Daniel Radcliffe was allergic to the glasses he had to wear to play Harry Potter.
- Angela Lansbury recorded the title song from Disney's *Beauty and the Beast* in one take.
- When she was nominated for a Best Supporting Actress award in 2003, Meryl Streep became the most Oscar-nominated actress in the history of cinema, with her a record-breaking 13th nomination. She has since gone on to be nominated more than 20 times.
- Hollywood actress Sandra Bullock speaks fluent German.
- Harrison Ford actually learned how to use a whip to play Indiana Jones.
- Christopher Lee, who played Saruman the White in the *Lord of the Rings* movies, had been a fan of the books for many years and could already speak Elvish.

WONDERFUL WORDS

LETTERS

- The word "alphabet" derives from the first two letters of the Greek alphabet—alpha and beta.
- On average, roughly one in every eight letters in written English is an E...
- ...but only one in every 500 is a Q!
- There are 26 letters in our alphabet, but there are 45 different sounds in our language.
- English has two one-letter words: A and I.
- X is the only letter of the alphabet that does not begin the name of a country.
- No one knows why our alphabet is in the order it's in.
- When the English alphabet was first written down more than 1,000 years ago, it had 29 letters.
- The symbol & used to be the 27th letter of the alphabet and was often listed after Z until the early 1900s.
- More English words begin with the letter S than any other letter.
- The last letter added to our alphabet was the letter J. It has only been part of our alphabet for around 500 years.

- The K in knee and knight used to be pronounced—the knee was "kuh-nee", and the knight was "kuh-night"!
- The word uncopyrightable contains no repeated letters.
- It is impossible to say the letter M without closing your lips.
- The capital letter B is the only English letter that contains entirely closed loops.
- The musical treble clef symbol, 𝄞, is actually an ornate form of the letter G...
- ...while the British pound symbol, £, is a form of the letter L.
- The letter M looks like a zigzagging line because historically it comes from an Egyptian hieroglyph that represented water with a zigzagging line!
- The letter R used to be known as the dog's letter because it sounds like a dog growling.
- Only four letters are allowed to be doubled at the start of English words: A (as in aardvark), E (as in eel), O (as in ooze), and L (as in llama).
- When written in capital letters, the world SWIMS still says SWIMS even when it's turned upside down!

- The word typewriter can be written using the keys found only on the top row of a computer keyboard.
- The words ewe (meaning a female sheep) and yew (a type of tree) are pronounced like "you" but are not spelled with a letter U!
- The words equation, dialogue, housemaid, favourite, behaviour, and boundaries all contain the letters A, E, I, O, and U (although UK spelling is needed for some of these words to make it so!).
- The string of letters - ough - can be pronounced at least seven different ways.
- The only standard English word that contains four letters Ks is knickknack.
- In the words, intestines, reappear, and signings, each letter appears exactly twice.
- In English, the letter you are most likely to see doubled is L.
- The most frequently used pair of letters in English is "th".
- Z didn't used to be the last letter of the alphabet—it used to be where our letter G now is!
- The dot on the letter i or j is called a tittle.

- Until around 1,000 years ago, it was common for words to be written all in capital letters with no spaces in between.
- A sentence that contains all 26 letters of the alphabet is called a pangram. "The quick brown fox jumps over the lazy dog" is one.
- If you were to write out every number in English in order—one, two, three, four, five, etc.—you wouldn't use a single letter B until you got to one billion!
- The word queue is still pronounced "kyoo" even when four of its letters have been removed: Q!
- V is the only letter of the alphabet that is never silent.
- From 1928 to 2013, it was illegal to use the letters Q, W, and X in Turkey.
- If you wrote out the names of every US state, you'd never need a letter Q...
- ...but you'd need a J for New Jersey, an X for Texas and New Mexico, and a Z for Arizona!

LANGUAGES

- There are more than 7,100 languages spoken in the world.
- English is spoken by one-quarter of all the people in the world...
- ...but over three-quarters of all the information stored on the world's computers is in English.
- French doesn't have any of its own words that begin with W. Any words in French that do start with W have been borrowed from other languages, like weekend, Wi-Fi, and web!
- A country where English is spoken is called an anglophone country. A francophone country speaks French, a hispanophone country speaks Spanish, and a lusophone country speaks Portuguese.
- The English language has been estimated to have more than 1 million words.
- The Hawaiian alphabet only has 13 letters.
- Around two-fifths of all the world's languages are never written down.
- In English, the word happy is used three times more often than the word sad.
- Norwegian, Danish, and Swedish are such similar languages that a Norwegian, a Dane, and

a Swede could hold a conversation together fairly easily.

- Anywhere from 30-45% of the words in an English dictionary have been borrowed from French.
- Swedish was only made the official language of Sweden in 2009.
- Switzerland has four official languages: French, Italian, German, and Romansch...
- ...but so that one language isn't given priority over the other, the country's name is written in Latin on its stamps and money!
- Some of the most commonly misspelled words in English include embarrassed, broccoli, accommodation, and calendar.
- The most commonly used word in the English language is "the"...
- ...while the most commonly used noun is "time".
- In English, the word "girl" used to mean "child," and so could be used for either boys or girls but is usually for girls!
- The country with the most French speakers isn't France—it's DR Congo in central Africa, where more than 100 million people speak French.
- Likewise, the country with the most Spanish speakers isn't Spain—it's Mexico.

- The Czech language contains a sound that is so difficult that some Czech speakers never learn how to say it properly. It is called the "raised alveolar non-sonorant trill," and is written in Czech with the letter ř.
- Xenoglossophobia is the fear of having to speak another language.
- The alphabet used to write the Khmer language of southeast Asia has 74 letters.
- The number of French speakers in the world has trebled in the past 100 years.
- There are more than 100,000 written Chinese characters.
- 25% of all the English you will ever read will be taken up by the words a, and, be, have, he, I, in, of, that, the, and to.
- Nahuatl is the language that was spoken by the Aztecs. It's from this language that English adopted the word chocolate.
- The Danish language has eight vowel letters, and 27 different vowel sounds.
- North Frisian is a language spoken by only around 10,000 people on some islands off the coast of Germany. It is the closest related language to English in the world.

- There is a special form of the Thai language reserved only for speaking to members of the Thai royal family.
- Vatican City is the only country in the world that still uses Latin as one of its languages. Even ATMs in the Vatican have an option to read the instructions in Roman Latin!
- English adopted the word robot from Czech...
- ...the word sauna from Finnish...
- ...the word kayak from the Inuit...
- ...and the word loot from Hindi!
- On average, one language dies—that is, ceases to be spoken—every two weeks.

WEIRD WORDS

- The longest word in most English dictionaries is pneumonoultramicroscopicsilicovolcanoconiosis—the name of the rare lung disease.
- Eidolism is the proper word for believing in ghosts.
- Oology is the scientific study of birds' eggs. It has the shortest name of any scientific subject.
- The small creases in the skin on the inside of your wrist are called rasceta.
- To sloum is to snooze or have a quick nap.
- Pothookery is bad handwriting.
- Something that is mesonoxian takes place at midnight.
- A wonderhorn is a collection of amazing things.
- To honeyfuggle someone is to trick them.
- Dutch pink is actually the name of a greenish shade of yellow.
- The opposite of postponing something is preponing it—bringing it forward in time.
- The loose feathers and dust that flies out of a cushion when it is hit are called the culf.
- The cosp is the handle of a spade.

- If you discalceate yourself then you remove your shoes.
- An eirmonger (an obsolete term) is someone who sells eggs.
- A murg is a heavy fall of snow.
- The shade below a tree is called the mogshade.
- The high-pitched chirping of ducks is called queepling.
- Because sunrises are often slightly softer in color in the mountains, the orange color of the sky at dawn is called alpenglow.
- In 19th century English, a waffle-frolic was a delicious meal.
- A slawterpooch is an awkward, ungainly person.
- If you're acrocomic then you have long hair.
- To punctulate something is to mark it with a dot.
- The ripple left on the surface of a body of water by an oar is called a capillary wave.
- Somewhere that is transmontane, is located on the opposite side of a mountain...
- ...while somewhere that is cismontane is located on the near side of a mountain!
- Something that is glairigenous produces slime.

- A telelogue is a conversation held over the phone.
- A line of moonlight reflected on the sea is called a moonglade.
- A melomane is someone who loves music.
- An abactor is someone who steals cows.
- To delimate something is to shave it or remove its rough edges.
- A thunderplump is a sudden, heavy downpour of rain.
- A tinctimutant creature is one that can change the color of its skin.
- The perforated bumps around the edge of a postage stamp are called the denticulation.
- Nurogenesis is the name of the process by which clouds are formed.
- Ataxophobia is the fear of untidiness...
- ...corvophobia is the fear of crows...
- ...haphephobia is the fear of being touched...
- ...and iatrophobia is the fear of going to the doctor.
- A whittleganger is a house guest who has outstayed their welcome.
- Someone who is startlesome is very easily frightened.

- Moles were once known as muddywants.
- The burned or blackened part of a candlewick is called the snaste.
- Someone who is novaturient wants things to change.
- A floscule is a tiny flower.
- An abecedarian is someone who is learning the alphabet.

WRITERS AND WRITING

- There are only six surviving records of William Shakespeare's signature—and he spells his name differently in each one!
- JK Rowling was originally turned down by 12 different publishers before *Harry Potter* was taken on by Bloomsbury Books...
- ...and *The Grinch* author Dr Seuss was turned down by 20!
- Charles Dickens was once so excited to see a friend of his in the street that he suddenly started dancing with her, accidentally knocked her over, and broke her arm!
- *The Little Mermaid* author Hans Christian Andersen once stayed at Charles Dickens' house for five weeks. (Dickens reportedly hated having him there!)
- Shakespeare was inspired to write a play called *The Tempest* after hearing the story of a real-life ship that had become wrecked during a hurricane in the Atlantic Ocean.
- JRR Tolkien, the author of *The Lord of the Rings*, and CS Lewis, the author of *The Lion, the Witch, and the Wardrobe*, were best friends.

- Shakespeare's father couldn't write his own name and used to sign official documents with a drawing of a pair of compasses.
- Tolkien wrote the entry for the word walrus for the *Oxford English Dictionary*.
- JK Rowling doesn't actually have a middle name. She began using a middle initial at the request of her publishers and chose K as a tribute to her grandmother, Kathleen.
- The first person in history to turn down a Nobel Prize was the French writer and philosopher Jean-Paul Sartre. He declined the Nobel Prize in Literature in 1964.
- Pippi Longstocking's full name is Pippilotta Delicatessa Windowshade Mackrelmint Ephraim's Daughter Longstocking.
- Dr Seuss had a closet full of hats that he would put on for inspiration...
- ...and he wrote *Green Eggs And Ham* after his publisher bet him that he couldn't write a story using only 50 different words.
- When he was a child, Roald Dahl, the author of *Charlie and the Chocolate Factory*, met Beatrix Potter, the creator of *Peter Rabbit*.
- In early drafts of *Charlie and the Chocolate Factory*, the Oompa-Loompas were named "Whipple-Scrumpets".

- *Alice in Wonderland* was once banned in China because animals should not talk.
- The *Goosebumps* series of stories have sold more than 350 million copies.
- Agatha Christie, the famous detective author, was a keen surfer.
- A copy of *The Very Hungry Caterpillar* is sold every minute somewhere in the world.
- *Peter Pan* was originally a play...
- ...and the villain Captain Hook was only added to the story to give the staff at the theatre more time to switch the sets around during the scenes!
- The earliest written record of the phrase "Knock, knock, who's there?" comes from Shakespeare's *Macbeth*.

SUPER SPORTS

SPORTS & SPORTSPEOPLE

- The FIFA World Cup is the most popular sports event in the world.
- The first recorded indoor ice hockey match was played in 1875.
- Until the 1940s, male swimmers often wore full-body swimming suits.
- One of the first great English cricketers was named Edward Lumpy Stevens. He died in 1819.
- Before golf tees were invented, golfers would hit the ball off a mound of sand.
- The first Boston Marathon was held in April 1897. It is the longest-running marathon race in the world.
- The Indianapolis Motor Speedway circuit in the town of Speedway in the USA has enough room for 350,000 spectators—that's almost four times the size of London's famous Wembley Stadium.
- In 2010, a single tennis match at Wimbledon lasted over 11 hours and had to be played over three days.
- The rules of America's Major League Baseball competition state that umpires have to wear black underpants!

- The longest recorded game of cricket took 12 days to complete.
- Basketball was invented by a youth club manager called James Naismith in 1891. Supposedly, he was asked to come up with an indoor game that the men at the club could play during the winter!
- Ice hockey pucks are frozen before a game to stop them from sticking to the ice.
- On average, a volleyball player will jump in the air around 300 times every game...
- ...while a football (soccer) player will run around 7 miles during the course of a single game.
- Most golf balls have anywhere between 300 and 500 dimples...
- ...but the average number is 336.
- On average, a baseball game takes three hours to complete but will see only 18 minutes of action.
- When basketball was first invented, the baskets were actual baskets, not hoops, and were sealed at the bottom. Whenever anyone scored, the ball would have to be retrieved from the basket before the game could restart!
- The lightest ball used in any competitive sport is the table tennis ball. It weighs barely 0.1 ounces.

- One hundred and eleven is considered an unlucky score in a game of cricket.
- Dribbling and dunking the ball in basketball were both originally banned.
- Technically, the heaviest ball used in competitive sport is an athletic shot put. In the men's event, the shot can weigh up to 16 lbs.
- The odds of being hit by a baseball while watching a game from the stands is 300,000 to 1.
- Served tennis balls and thrown baseball pitches move through the air faster than a cheetah can run.
- The first person in recorded history to run a mile in under four minutes was the British athlete Roger Banister in 1954. His record time of 3:59.4 only stood for 46 days before it was broken again; today, more than 1,600 athletes have now broken the four-minute mark.
- Warmed water is frozen to make the ice on an ice hockey rink because it freezes clearer than cold water.
- Cricket bats are always made of willow.
- Aside from golf, polo has the largest playing area of any competitive ball sport because it

is played on horseback. A standard polo field is 300 yards long and 160 yards wide.

- The creator of Sherlock Holmes, Arthur Conan Doyle, was a keen bodybuilder and once judged a bodybuilding competition held at the Royal Albert Hall in London.
- Golf balls were originally made of feathers. Basically, the feathery was a leather sack filled with boiled goose feathers, then stitched up and painted.
- In 2018, 115,000 attended a single baseball game in Los Angeles, California.
- There are playing positions in a game of cricket called silly mid-on, deep square leg, cow corner, deep backward point, fly slip, and silly point.

THE OLYMPIC GAMES

- When all the countries enter the Olympic stadium during the opening ceremony, the first country is always Greece—because historically, that's where the Olympics started.
- The host country is always last to enter the arena during the opening ceremony.
- All the other countries arrive alphabetically—which has been the tradition for Olympic opening ceremonies since 1928!
- The tiny European country of Liechtenstein has competed in more Olympic Games without ever winning a medal than any other unsuccessful country.
- At the 1904 Olympics, American gymnast George Eyser won six medals in one day, despite having a wooden leg!
- At the 1976 Olympic Games in Montreal, the Olympic flame was accidentally put out by heavy rain. One of the officials had to relight it with a cigarette lighter!
- The 1908 Olympics were the first Games at which the swimming event took place in a swimming pool. Before then, swimming had been raced on seas, rivers, and lakes.

- The three-level podium on which winning Olympic athletes stand was introduced in 1932.
- In 1924, Paris became the first city in the world to host the Olympic Games twice...
- ...while in 2012, London became the first city to host the Games three times!
- The 1968 Mexico City Games were the first broadcast on television in color.
- More world records were broken at the 2008 Beijing Olympics than at any other time in history.
- The 1928 Amsterdam Olympics were meant to be opened by the Queen of the Netherlands, Wilhelmina, but she ended up going on holiday and leaving her husband to do it!
- In 1948, Dutch sprinter Fanny Blankers-Koen—who was 30 years old and had two children—defied all expectations and won four gold medals, earning herself the nickname "The Flying Housewife!"
- Vertical rope climbing was an event at the Olympic Games until 1932...
- ...while tug-of-war was an Olympic event until 1920.
- Olympic gold medals aren't solid gold—they're silver, coated in a thin layer of gold.

- The official mascot of the 1932 Olympics was a black Scottish terrier dog called Smoky.
- When the Olympics were held in Melbourne in 1956, Australia's strict quarantine laws meant that horses could not enter the country to take part in equestrian events. So instead, the horse-riding events were held five months earlier in Sweden!
- The five colors on the Olympic flag—yellow, green, red, black, and blue—were chosen because at least one of them appears somewhere on every flag in the world.
- The first Asian nation to compete in the Olympic Games was Japan in 1912.
- When it was discovered that the only teams who had entered the dinghy sailing event at the 1920 Olympic Games in Antwerp were Dutch, the event was held across the border in the Netherlands to save them traveling to Belgium!
- US swimmer Michael Phelps has won 28 Olympic medals—Phelps also holds the all-time records for Olympic gold medals, Olympic gold medals in individual events, and Olympic medals in individual events.
- ...of which 23 are gold!
- The African country of Northern Rhodesia declared its independence during the 1964

Olympics in Tokyo. As such it became the first and only country in sporting history to start the Olympics under one name and leave under another: Zambia.

- Synchronized swimming has only been an Olympic event since 1984.
- At the 1904 Olympics, only two teams competed in the football (soccer) competition. In the end, Canada beat the United States to take the gold medal!
- The parking sign was invented for the 1928 Amsterdam Olympics.
- During the steeplechase race at the 1932 Olympics, the judge lost count and the race ran for an extra lap. Instead of 1.86 miles, it was contested over 2.15 miles.
- When the Olympics were held in Mexico City in 1968, the Olympic flame was carried across the Atlantic Ocean from Greece, retracing Christopher Columbus' route to North America.
- The 2010 Winter Olympic ice hockey final was watched by 80% of the population of Canada.
- At the 2004 Olympics in Athens, twin brothers Paul and Morgan Hamm won gold and silver medals in gymnastics.

GAMES AND PASTIMES

- Scrabble was originally called Lexico.
- The longest game of Monopoly ever recorded took 70 days.
- The earliest paper playing cards were originally made in China.
- In some countries, the diamonds in a pack of cards are replaced with gold.
- It is possible to solve a Rubik's cube in 20 moves.
- The world's first crossword puzzle was called a wordcross puzzle.
- In the Polish version of Scrabble, Z is worth one point.
- The person you operate on in the game Operation is called Cavity Sam.
- ...the person who has been killed at the start of a game of Cluedo is called Mr. Boddy...
- ...and the police officer who sends you to jail in a game of Monopoly is called Officer Edgar Mallory.
- More Monopoly money is printed in the United States each year than real cash.

- The best set of letters to have in a game of Scrabble is AEINRST. They can be arranged to spell nine different words, including retains, nastier, retinas, and stainer.
- There are more ways of arranging the cards in a deck of cards than there are stars in our galaxy.
- The highest-scoring word in a game of Scrabble is potentially the 15-letter chemical term oxyphenbutazone. It would need to be played across the whole board but would score 1,782 points!
- There are 52 cards in a standard deck of playing cards...
- ...and coincidentally, a total of 52 letters in the words ace, king, queen, jack, ten, nine, eight, seven, six, five, four, three, and two!
- The word "twelve" would score 12 points in a game of Scrabble.
- Some card games have a rule that states the queen card outranks the king card, but only when the ruling British monarch is a queen as well!
- Jazz is supposedly the hardest word to guess in a game of hangman.

- It is theoretically possible to bankrupt your opponent in a game of Monopoly within two turns.
- There is around a 15% chance that the first seven letters picked at the start of a game of Scrabble will spell a word.
- Someone who collects stamps is called a philatelist...
- ...while someone who collects teddy bears is an arctophile...
- ...a fan of crosswords is a cruciverbalist...
- ...and a deltiologist is a collector of postcards.
- Chinese checkers aren't checkers and don't come from China. The game was invented in Germany in 1892.

EVERYTHING & EVERYWHERE

POTLUCK

- Ketchup and Coca-Cola were once marketed as medicine.
- In 1996, scientists successfully cloned a sheep called Dolly.
- Nobody knows what Noah's wife's name was in the Bible.
- The national animal of Scotland is the unicorn.
- It was once illegal to flirt in New York City. Anyone caught looking romantically at someone else could be fined $25.
- St Barbara is the patron saint of fireworks and firefighters.
- Flies can't hear their own buzz.
- According to the *Guinness Book of Records*, "the sixth sick sheikh's sixth sheep's sick" is the hardest tongue twister in the English language.
- The most frequently struck key on a computer keyboard is the space bar.
- T-shirts are so called because they look like the letter T!
- Leotards are named after a French trapeze artist called Jules Léotard.

- In 1964, a California student named Randy Gardner stayed awake for 11 days.
- The longest-lived character in the Bible is Methuselah. He supposedly lived to be 969 years old.
- Only three countries in the world do not use the metric system of measurements: Liberia in Africa, Myanmar in southeast Asia, and the United States.
- Some scientists think that tickling was originally a defense mechanism.
- British judges wear wigs because the tradition started at a time when ornate wigs were fashionable among prominent members of society. Although the fashion did not last, the legal tradition has!
- Around one-fifth to one-half of all household dust is made from skin.
- Cleveland, Ohio, was originally called Cleaveland, with an A. The letter was removed so that the city's name would better fit on the front of the local newspaper.
- There are more than 600,000 bridges in the United States, 40% of which have been standing for more than 50 years.
- Lemons float in water, but limes sink.

- William Shakespeare's father was the official ale taster of Stratford. Part of his job involved sitting in a pool of ale wearing leather trousers to see how sticky it became.
- The small pocket inside the larger pocket on the front of a pair of jeans was originally intended to hold a pocket watch.
- Pineapples grow on the ground.
- As well as meaning to excite someone, to thrill can also mean to pierce a hole in something...
- ...which makes your nostrils literally your "nose-thrills!"
- Fashion retailer H&M stands for Hennes & Mauritz—the name of two stores that combined to form the brand in 1968.
- Mayonnaise is named after the port of Mahon on the Spanish island of Minorca.
- The first ever tweet said, "just setting up my twttr."
- There are 32,000 branches of Starbucks around the world, in 80 different countries.
- The Eiffel Tower was only meant to be a temporary attraction and was intended to be taken down and scrapped. It was only allowed to remain standing because it made the perfect site for a long-range radio antenna during the First World War!

- ...which is just as well, because it remained the tallest manmade structure on the planet for the following 40 years.
- In 19th century England, trousers were nicknamed "sit-upons".
- Panama hats are actually from Ecuador.
- In medieval Switzerland, a chicken was mistakenly identified as a rooster and was tried as a witch when it was found to have laid an egg.
- In Canada, letters to Santa Claus can be sent to the postal code HOH OHO.
- The tango dance was originally intended to be a dance between two men.

CONCLUSION

And with our 1,272nd fact, our list of Super Interesting Facts is complete!

So, what have we learned along the way?

Well, we now know just how busy a bee has to be to make honey—and how many flowers might have been involved in the jar on the shelf in your kitchen!

We know how much money we would need to buy the world's most expensive painting.

We know how far we'd have to go to travel as far as the furthest-flying bird—and how far we'd have to go to visit the Sun!

(Though if we wanted to experience really hot temperatures, there are plenty of places on Earth where we could find them!)

We have found out a lot more besides that, of course. What was your favorite Super Interesting Fact?